THE TRINITY

THE TRINITY

KARL RAHNER

Translated by Joseph Donceel

Introduction, index, and glossary by
Catherine Mowry LaCugna

A Crossroad Herder Book
The Crossroad Publishing Company
New York

This printing: 1999

The Crossroad Publishing Company
370 Lexington Avenue, New York, NY 10017

Original edition: "Der dreifaltige Gott als transzendeter Urgrund
der Heilsgeschichte," in *Die Heilsgeschichte vor Christus,* volume 2 of
Mysterium Salutis, Grundriss heilsgeschichtlicher Dogmatik

Nihil obstat: Leo J. Steady, Censor Librorum
Imprimatur: ✠ Robert F. Joyce, Bishop of Burlington
November 14, 1969

Printed in the United States of America

Library of Congress Cataloging-in-Publication Data

Rahner, Karl, 1904 –
   [Dreifaltige Gott als transzendenter Urgrund der
   Heilsgeschichte. English]
   The Trinity / Karl Rahner ; translated by Joseph Donceel ;
   introduction, index, and glossary by Catherine Mowry LaCugna.
      p.   cm.
   Includes bibliographical references and index.
   ISBN 0–8245–1627–3 (pbk.)
   1. Trinity.   I. Title.
BT 111.2.R31   1997
231'.044—dc21   96–51964
                                                            CIP

CONTENTS

INTRODUCTION

By the end of the Second Vatican Council (1962-65) a new spirit was blowing in the church, not just with respect to the Council's vision of the renewal of church life. The documents of Vatican II were themselves the fruit of innovative theological thinking and opened the door to a fresh way of thinking about the nature of theology and the arrangement of theological themes. After the Council, the great theologians who shaped its vision wrote influential books and articles that parlayed the work of the Council into a massive rethinking of every aspect of theology. Karl Rahner (1904-84) was particularly prolific, and immediately attracted a multinational following.

Rahner saw that Vatican II was setting free Catholicism from the confines of neo-scholasticism. Medieval scholasticism was a system of inquiry that relied on Aristotelian logic and metaphysics to probe theological topics, and used the method of *quaestio* and *disputatio* to explore theological issues. Neo-scholasticism, in contrast, was an effort to retrieve the medieval synthesis to overcome the severe challenges posed to Christianity by the Enlightenment. Neo-scholasticism emerged after 1840 as a somewhat rigid and unimaginative simplification of the richness and diversity of medieval theologies. Rahner, like most theologians at Vatican II, had been trained in this "school theology." But by the time of Vatican II, neo-scholasticism was widely criticized as unhistorical, ill-equipped to deal with the modern turn to the subject, out of touch with modern science, and overly focused on lifeless concepts as opposed to experience. Moreover, its adherents aimed at a total monopoly, excluding all other theologies, old and new. In the years immediately preceding Vatican II, some theologians had already begun to move away from the neo-scholastic way of arranging and approaching the major themes of theology.

The Trinity originally appeared thirty years ago in Mysterium Salutis, a multi-volume systematic theology written in German and produced from 1967-1976 by theologians prominent at Vatican II. As soon as the first volume appeared, the publishers planned English, Spanish, and French translations. The British and American editors planned a new format. The large volumes would appear in small books written by different authors, corresponding to the segments in the volumes. Only three of these sections materialized in English books, one of which is The Trinity. Further translations of Mysterium Salutis into English were soon discontinued.

The structure of The Trinity reflects Rahner's dialogue with neo-scholasticism. It is characteristic of Rahner's work in general to give the neo-scholastic position and then contrast it to his own. The Trinity begins with a discussion of the traditional medieval and neo-scholastic structure of the treatise, On the Triune God, as well as of the traditional way of formulating the doctrines of God (divine incomprehensibility), Christ (Incarnation), and the Holy Spirit (grace). Part II comprises a subtle and sophisticated hermeneutics of magisterial statements, along with a consideration of traditional trinitarian vocabulary. Part III contains Rahner's own theology of the Trinity, a synthesis of early patristic (Greek) and Augustinian-Thomistic (Latin) theologies, advanced beyond the categories of neo-scholasticism and informed by the distinctively modern concerns of history, personhood, subjectivity, and relationality.

In Part I Rahner expresses his dismay at the inadequate theologies of Incarnation and grace that characterized neo-scholasticism in the twentieth century. They prevented the formulation of a viable and intelligible doctrine of the Trinity that could be connected with Christian faith, practice, and spirituality. Indeed, Rahner argued that the chief reason the doctrine of the Trinity had become irrelevant was because neo-scholasticism had produced a "unitarian" christology and theology of grace. Hence Rahner's oft-cited remark that "Christians are, in their practical life, almost mere 'monotheists'....[S]hould the doctrine of the Trinity have to be dropped as false, the major part of religious literature could well remain virtually unchanged" (10-11).

Rahner bemoans the isolation of the doctrine of the Trinity from Christian life and spirituality, as well as its separation from other doctrines within neo-scholastic textbooks. He is also critical of the Thomistic treatment of God under two treatises, "On the One God" (*De Deo Uno*) and "On the Triune God" (*De Deo Trino*). The "normal" procedure, he writes, would be to begin with ὁ Θεός, the person of the Father, in conformity to the Bible, early creeds, liturgical practice, and Greek patristic theology. But in the Latin West, Thomas Aquinas's approach, as taken over by neo-scholasticism, hardened the legitimate distinction between the treatises into two separate tracts, thereby making it possible for Christian theology to treat, first, God's unity, the divine essence, divine attributes, and divine names, and only secondarily consider matters distinctive to the divine persons (processions, relations, persons, *propria*, missions). In the neo-scholastic arrangement, a false disjunction between faith and reason could be read between the lines: the existence and oneness of God could be discerned by reason, the divine persons only by revelation. The tract on the Trinity seemed, as Rahner said, not essential to Christian faith and certainly not first in the order of experience.

The neo-scholastic dogmatic structure made the tract on the Trinity impermeable to other relevant themes (such as soteriology) and, most unfortunate of all, presented a trinitarian theology disconnected from the revelation and the experience of Father, Son, and Spirit in salvation history. Trinitarian theology became a purely speculative endeavor, of interest to precious few, unintelligible to the vast majority. Hence the misleading commonplace that "We cannot explain anything about the doctrine of the Trinity since it is a mystery." (God is mystery, to be sure; the doctrine is complex but not the same as the Mystery.) And so, generations of Christians were taught virtually nothing about this central truth of the Christian faith, except that it was enshrouded in mystery and in any case had no bearing on living out one's faith.

In order to rejoin Christian practice and the doctrine of the Trinity, Rahner perceived it necessary to reappropriate the pre-Augustinian, Greek theology of God according to which God the Father is *fontalis*, the source of divinity for both Son and Spirit. The invisible, incomprehensible God comes to humanity in Christ by the power of the Holy Spirit. God's self-communication (*selbst-Mitteilen*) is necessarily triune and constitutes salvation history to be what it is: the total offer of God's self through Christ to the human being who is created as the recipient of the self-communication of God, and who is made capable by the Spirit of receiving God's free gift. Rahner recognized that the only way to ensure that the doctrine of the Trinity and the doctrine of salvation are seen as one and the same was to adhere to the biblical, creedal, liturgical, and Greek emphasis on the diversity of the divine persons in our salvation.

In contrast, in the Latin West, Augustine and his followers began their doctrine of the Trinity with the unity of the divine essence, and with a certain separation of eternal processions and historical missions. This approach raised the specter of a creeping monism that de-emphasized the diversity of the divine persons as attested in the biblical order of salvation history and in our experience of God through Christ in the Spirit. Augustine saw the divine processions unfolding within each human soul where the powers of memory, intellect, and will mirror God's triune life. This trajectory, however insightful in its own right for its recognition of the image of the Trinity in the human soul, weighted anthropology over the events in salvation history and favored the unity of divine essence over the diversity of divine persons. Father, Son, and Spirit were conceived in intra-divine terms, with the emphasis on their absolute equality and perfect unity, but at the cost of a lively sense of the uniqueness of each divine person's activity in salvation history. The axiom "All the works of God *ad extra* are one" encapsulates Augustine's emphasis on divine unity. It is true indeed that Father, Son, and Holy Spirit act always together; every act for our salvation is a trinitarian act. But any differences among the persons become almost imperceptible. The doctrine of appropriations, by which activities in salvation history are attributed to a divine person (the Father creates, Son redeems, Spirit sanctifies), compensates for the de-emphasis on the concrete manifestations of God's providential plan in history.

Thomas Aquinas adapted Augustine's theo-psychology of the soul and produced a profound theology of the analogy between the eternal Begetting of the Word and Breathing forth of the Spirit, and the two human activities of knowing and loving. But neo-scholasticism distorted this positive theme of Augustinian and medieval theology and relegated the divine persons to an "intra-divine" sphere, a Trinity of persons quite unrelated to us. Rahner laments that "...all these statements [of the dogmatic manuals] *say explicitly* in cold print that we ourselves have nothing to do with the mystery of the Holy Trinity except to know something 'about it' through revelation" (14). Even if an appeal is made to the beatific vision in which we shall see God "face to face," Rahner continues, "How can the contemplation of any reality, even of the loftiest reality, beatify us if intrinsically it is absolutely *unrelated* to us in any way?" (15).

Just as neo-scholasticism had failed to be thoroughly trinitarian in its theology of God by reducing any sense of the salvific activity of the unique divine persons "for us and for our salvation," the same incoherency could be observed in its christology (Jesus Christ) and theology of grace (Holy Spirit). Because of the century or so of neo-scholastic influence on Christian consciousness, Christians in general and even many Christian theologians, Rahner notes, are unaware that God as such did not become incarnate but only the second divine person. Rahner is critical of all those, including Thomas Aquinas (cf. *Summa Theologiae* III, q. 23, a. 2), who took the position that *any* divine person could have become incarnate. If that were true, Rahner reasons, then the incarnation of the Son would tell us nothing about the unique personal identity of the Son in his mission of Incarnation, nor about the eternally Begotten Son ("procession"). Jesus Christ is not God in general but the Incarnate Word. Only the Logos became human. Therefore there is at least one mission, one instance in salvation history, that is not just appropriated to the Son but is proper to him (*proprium*) (23).

Similarly, the graced relationship between God and humanity was thought of in terms of created grace, a grace given to the human person by God's efficient causality and appropriated to the Holy Spirit. Aristotle had postulated four causes: formal, material, efficient, and final. According to the neo-scholastics, grace—true divine presence—had to fit one of Aristotle's categories. Grace could not be a *formal* cause, since this would obliterate the ontological distinction between God and the human person (Creator and creature would be the same in being). The neo-scholastics settled on efficient causality, even though this meant that God's relationship to the creature in grace was extrinsic. This certainly added to the impression that the triune God is not "really" related to us. Further, while God's presence in grace is the work of the divine persons together, the neoscholastics appropriated grace to the Holy Spirit instead of seeing grace as an indwelling of the triune God.

Rahner passed beyond the dominance of actual grace as a transitional effect of the Spirit and built his theology of grace around the idea of quasi-formal causality. He retains the Aristotelian causal framework but amends it by restoring the category of quasi-formal (found in a very few places in Aquinas). Quasi-formal means something more than efficient, less than formal causality. The indwelling of the divine persons in grace makes the graced person as close to God as possible without erasing the ontological difference between God and creature. Grace is truly God as such, and does affect the creature ontologically, but grace does not remove the creatureliness of the human being. This is a contemporary version of the Eastern theology of deification based on 2 Peter 3:4: God makes us "partakers of the divine nature" not by nature but by grace. Clearly Rahner's ontology (and causality) is no longer strictly Aristotelian.

The discussion of Incarnation and grace constitutes Rahner's effort to reconnect the doctrine of the Trinity with the doctrine of salvation, and in the process to reestablish links among trinitarian theology, christology and soteriology, and pneumatology, and especially between *De Deo Uno* and *De Deo Trino*. Incarnation and grace are offered as "dogmatic proof" of Rahner's axiom: "The 'economic' Trinity is the 'immanent' Trinity, and vice versa" (22).

The economic Trinity refers to God's activity and presence in salvation history, particularly the missions of Son and Spirit in redemption and deification. Immanent Trinity, for Rahner, refers to the divine persons in relationship to one another "within"

God. Rahner's theology of God is based on the premise that God is by nature self-communicating: Father to Son and Spirit. The economic Trinity manifests the perpetual self-communication of God under the conditions of time and history, hence in the missions of Christ and the Spirit. The identity of "economic" and "immanent" Trinity means that God truly and completely gives God's self to the creature without remainder, and what is given in the economy of salvation *is* God as such. Both the distinction and the identity between the economic and immanent Trinity are conceptual, not ontological. There is only one trinitarian self-communication, which has both eternal and temporal aspects. Rahner does not mean, as in a tautology, that eternal and temporal realms are strictly identical, only that no gap may be inserted (as in neo-scholasticism) between "God" and "God for us." Missions and processions are the same reality under different aspects. The eternal begetting of the Son is the eternal ground of the sending of the Son in the Incarnation. Likewise with the Holy Spirit. What distinguishes Rahner's axiom from neo-scholasticism is that he derives the axiom not from *a priori* principles but from salvation history.

More than any other feature of this book, Rahner's axiom prompted wide commentary and some criticism. While there has been general agreement with the basic meaning of the axiom (God truly is as God reveals God's self to be, and *vice versa*), many theologians, and from different confessional traditions, have questioned whether there can be a *strict* identity between "economic" and "immanent" Trinity. Must there not be a certain asymmetry between God *"in se"* and God *"pro nobis"*? Rahner certainly did not intend to promote pantheism. Nor did he mean the axiom to license speculation on the immanent Trinity apart from the economy of salvation history.

If the axiom is taken to describe an ontological state of affairs, then the critics are correct to insist that there remain some essential difference between the being of the triune God and the being of the creature (though few have successfully maintained the distinction without abrogating the essential relatedness of God and creature). Even if an asymmetry is acknowledged, it does not follow that there is a second Trinity, an immanent Trinity, that can be treated in the manner of neo-scholasticism, independently of God's self-revelation in salvation history. There is only one divine self-communication, only *one* trinity of persons. If Rahner's axiom is construed ontologically, then it clearly requires qualification, since, as it stands, it fails to shed light on an adequate way to maintain both the ontological difference between God and creation, *and* the ontological relatedness of God to creation.

On a somewhat different plane, the axiom does not provide any hints about how to maintain the freedom of God's trinitarian self-communication. Many theologians who insist on an ontological difference between "economic" and "immanent" Trinity do so because they see no other way to preserve God's freedom "not to create." God may be self-communicating *ad intra*, but God need not bestow God's self *ad extra* (creation being one moment of God's self-communication). These issues continue to be under discussion among theologians, and Rahner's axiom really does not help clarify them. But then, divine freedom was not the issue around which he formulated the axiom. This is why it is more accurate to see the axiom as a methodological rather than ontological insight: the order of theological knowledge must adhere to the historical form of God's self-communication in Christ and the Spirit. Knowledge of God takes place through Christ and the Holy Spirit, according to the order (*taxis*) of the divine missions. However scholars choose to amend Rahner's axiom, this much must be preserved: the essential connection

between the doctrine of God and soteriology, and the unaccepti-
bility of the long-standing isolation of the doctrine of the Trinity
from the rest of theology.

Rahner's analysis in Part II of the magisterium's teaching on
the doctrine of the Trinity is masterful and theologically fruitful,
even though its presence and proportions might strike some as
puzzling. Most theologians today would be unlikely to devote a
significant portion of a book to review magisterial statements on
a particular topic. Yet it was important to Rahner, first, to situate
his efforts in continuity with traditional theology "to make sure
that this [new] theology is the theology of the Church" (49); second, to show that his own theology of the Trinity is at least not
ruled out by previous church teaching. Rahner analyzes the con-
troverted terms: person, substance, essence, nature, unity. This is
followed by a summary of magisterial teaching on God the
Father, the Unoriginate Origin of the Son; on the Son who is Begotten from the Father's substance; on the Holy Spirit who
bestows on us the gift of the Father through the Son and also
makes it possible for us to accept this self-communication.
Rahner also treats dogmatic statements on the relations among
the divine persons: for instance, the relationship between person
and nature; the doctrine of appropriations; and predications
made of the divine essence as distinct from those made of divine
persons.

The result is far more than a recitation of Denzinger (a collection of church documents). Rahner gives the reader an apprecia-
tion of the richness of the dogmatic tradition, as well as of the
critical need for sustained theological interpretation and expan-
sion of the statements of the magisterium. Like most dogmatic
definitions, these speak sparingly and mostly by way of negation,
ruling out certain interpretations rather than specifying their
application or meaning. It falls to the theologian to translate the
essential truths being safeguarded in the dogmatic definitions.

One of the hallmarks of Catholic theology is to rethink and restate essential truths in a contemporary idiom while staying in continuity with Tradition. Rahner is an excellent guide here, even if his diligence might seem out of the ordinary to many today.

In Part III Rahner develops his own theology of the Trinity. Rahner was unsympathetic to Augustine's focus on interiority and to the so-called psychological analogy for the divine persons. Instead he favored Greek patristic theology, which flowed from the biblical narratives and the liturgical enactment of Christian faith. Rahner was, nonetheless, profoundly influenced by Augustine and Thomas Aquinas. He takes up the theme of the two processions of Son and Spirit and applies it *not to the soul but to salvation history itself.* This was a brilliant way to interweave the two heritages of East and West.

God's self-communication is expressed both eternally and temporally in two modalities: Word and Spirit. This obviously correlates with the two spiritual activities of knowing and loving. But rather than follow Augustine and begin with a philosophical understanding of knowledge and love and then speculatively apply these concepts to the Trinity, *Rahner maps the two-foldness of divine self-communication onto salvation history.* He proposes the quadriform: Origin–Future; History–Transcendence; Invitation–Acceptance; Knowledge–Love. The first set of terms forms an inner unity, as does the second. God's self-communication means, on the one hand, the absolutely free gift of God to the human person, mediated by Christ and the Spirit. At the same time, God's self-communication brings into existence the very creature who is thereby constituted the recipient. The existence of a suitable addressee is the condition for the possibility of the divine self-communication. Just as the human nature of Christ comes into existence when the Logos utters itself outwards, so the four double aspects of God's self-communication come into being when the creature is constituted as the recipient of God's self-gift. The creature is not constituted as the appropriate recipient in some *interior* way, as with Augustine, but in a *historical* way. Divine self-communication always takes place according to a trinitarian pattern in history: the Father communicates the divine essence by uttering the Son in the Incarnation and bestowing the Spirit who brings about our response through grace.

The two modalities of God's self-communication, Word and Spirit, constitute salvation history in truth and as love. This, Rahner says, is the content of the economic Trinity which is, in its turn, the foundation for the immanent Trinity. The two-fold distinction of persons in salvation history "must belong to God 'in himself'" (100), else there can be no true *self*-communication.

Rahner's sustained reflection on God's self-communication in Christ and the Spirit lays the groundwork for his proposal regarding the nature of personhood. Person is obviously the key term in the doctrine of the Trinity (although, as Rahner observes, one could formulate a theology of the Trinity without it). It has always had many meanings. Boethius, for example, defined person as "an individual substance of a rational nature," Thomas Aquinas as "subsistent relation." In today's post-Cartesian world, person connotes a discrete center of consciousness, an individual center of freedom and action. Three such centers would amount to three gods. Thus it may well be misleading to recite the formula, "one God, three persons" unless the term person is shed of its individualistic connotations.

Rather than derive a definition of person from philosophy or psychology or some other discipline, the proper theological approach, Rahner says, would be to define a divine person on the basis of salvation history where we experience Father, Son, and Spirit each as God. Each divine person is a person in an absolutely unique way. The person of the Father is to be the Unbegotten Begetter, who is radically different from the person of the Son, who is Begotten and Incarnate. To say three persons and mean it univocally would be erroneous.

Moreover, the relationship between person and nature has never been easy to balance. At the Council of Nicaea (325), *hypostasis* and *ousia* were used interchangeably; one could say three persons or three substances. The Cappadocians (fourth century) clarified the terminology so that *ousia* (Latin: *substantia*) meant only substance, and *hypostasis* (Latin: *subsistentia*) only person. Augustine was fully justified, after examining the differences between Greek and Latin terms still to ask, "Three what?" He reasoned that since in God there are neither division nor accidents, the divine persons must be identical with the divine substance. The Father is God, the Son is God, the Spirit is God, yet there is only one God. The divine essence cannot be multiplied, nor can divine perfections (for example, wisdom, goodness) nor anything else belonging to the divine nature. Only persons can be plural.

Still, a distinction must be preserved between person and nature. Typically this was done by defining person in terms of *relation*. The Greek fathers defined a divine person as a relation of origin, the "from whom" a person comes. The Father is Unbegotten (from no one), the Son Begotten (from the Father), the Spirit Proceeding (from the Father [through the Son]). Many in the Latin tradition, especially Thomas Aquinas, defined person in terms of relations of opposition. The Father is Father of the Son (Begetter), the Son is Begotten of the Father, the Spirit is Spirated by Father and Son. An exaggerated version of either tradition would lead to modalism or tritheism.

Rahner takes a new approach. He notes Karl Barth's definition of person as a "mode of being," but prefers "distinct manner of subsisting." This is a technically precise definition because it captures both the diversity of the persons and their shared God-ness. The medievals and neo-scholastics used *individuum subsistens*, but Rahner's interpretation of it is new. Properly understood, the definition precludes the tendency of Latin theology to conceive of "God" or "Godhead" prior to the concrete person of the Father. How so? Rahner relies on Greek theology according to which the Father is God; the Father is *fontalis*, the font and origin of divinity from whom Son and Spirit proceed. The unity of the divine persons is found not in a common essence (as with Augustine or Thomas) but in the person of the Father and in the perichoretic interrelatedness of the divine persons. The Father always has a certain priority (neither ontological nor chronological) over Son and Spirit. Indeed, Rahner explicitly states that the *Father* is the self-communicating One, through Christ and the Spirit. The *Father* communicates *as God*, and communicates the divine essence as such. The Father is both Unbegotten and Begetter; the Father is not the result of a prior communication, and the Father is the supremely and freely self-communicating God.

All this is another way of saying that Rahner follows Greek theology by using person (the person of the Father), not substance (shared divine essence), as the ultimate ontological category. Had Rahner adhered to the neo-scholastic paradigm, he would have been unable to overcome the sense of a divine essence on the verge of becoming a fourth person. Nor would he have been able to escape a theology ultimately headed toward unitarianism. As a speculative achievement, "distinct manner of subsisting" is an adroit rendering of the many senses of the tradition. Rahner contends that his definition requires neither a specifically Latin nor Greek trinitarian theology. Yet, as many have noted, the concept is not especially easy to explain and certainly not useful for preaching. Theological definitions of person will continue to evolve, as they should. Personhood will remain notoriously difficult to define precisely, but that may be a good reminder that no one concept is up to the task of defining the ineffable mystery of God.

To the casual observer *The Trinity* may appear to be just more speculation on a recondite matter unrelated to Christian life and practice. Admittedly, the text is not always easy to read, and it presupposes some acquaintance with the intricate theories of the dogmatic manuals and the technical language of trinitarian doctrine. Nonetheless, the reprinting of *The Trinity* is a very happy occasion. Rahner's book launched one of the most significant theological developments of the last few decades: the restoration of the doctrine of the Trinity to its rightful place at the center of Christian faith. His thesis on the identity of "economic" and "immanent" Trinity continues to inspire scholars to articulate the implications of thinking together the doctrine of God and the doctrine of salvation. Journals and books are full of efforts to link the doctrine of the Trinity with the nature and mission of the church, the efficacy of the sacraments, the universal presence of the Spirit, dialogue with other religions, ecumenism, spirituality and mysticism, liberation and feminist theologies, not to mention christology and pneumatology proper. At this time of great ferment in Christian theology, it is a boon to have Rahner's seminal work available once again. Perhaps the greatest tribute to Rahner would be to note that because of his book and the theological discussions that continue to follow, no longer is it true that if the doctrine of the Trinity were to be "dropped as false, the major part of religious literature could well remain virtually unchanged" (10-11).

Catherine Mowry LaCugna
Advent, 1996

IMPORTANT TERMS

Appropriations, Doctrine of. Since the three divine persons share equally in the divine essence, all act together in salvation history: "The operations of the Trinity *ad extra* are one"(Council of Florence, 1441-42). Yet actions may be attributed (or "appropriated") to particular divine persons where suitable (the Father creates, the Son redeems, the Spirit sanctifies) without denying that all three persons equally share the act.

Beatific Vision. The proper end of the human person, eternal union with God "face to face."

Begotten. Greek *gennetos* (born). Unique property of the Son, eternally generated by the Father.

Economy (of salvation). God's providential plan of salvation; God's management and dispensation of grace.

Economic Trinity. The divine persons as they are revealed and act in salvation history.

Grace, Created. Supernatural gifts given by God beyond the natural capacity of human beings. Created grace is the result of God's free self-communication in Word and Spirit, and is available to all persons.

1

Grace, Uncreated. The very life of the triune God, given as divine self-communication.

Hypostasis. Greek term meaning "something with a concrete existence"; in Trinitarian theology, "person" (Latin *subsistentia* or *persona*). By the end of the fourth century, *hypostasis* is used as a synonym for a single, concrete instance of *ousia* (nature) *Hypostasis* refers to what is distinct, *ousia* to what is shared in God. According to the classic Trinitarian formula, God exists as three *hypostases*, one *ousia*, that is, as three persons in one substance or nature. Father, Son, and Spirit are each unique *hypostases*; together they are one divinity. See also **Notion**.

Immanent Trinity. The divine persons with respect to one another.

Logical Explanation. A set of coherent ideas that makes the understanding of a reality or an idea more precise in and of itself, independently of reference to extrinsic, even if related, circumstances. According to Rahner, person and essence are logical explanations. The meaning of these concepts is derived from an original faith experience of the diverse divine persons along with their unity in the economy of salvation. Thus the statement "one God (essence, substance) in three persons." Compare **Ontic Explanation**.

Mystery, God as. Mystery is attributed to God not because of the poverty of the human intellect, but because it belongs to the nature of God. The incomprehensible God is nonetheless present to the human person in his or her intrinsic openness to the infinite.

Neo-scholasticism. Developing in the mid-nineteenth century and continuing as the predominant form of theology until the Second Vatican Council, neo-scholasticism combined the thought of Thomas Aquinas with elements drawn from other thinkers both medieval and modern, constituting a variant of Thomism profoundly shaped by modern rationalism.

Notion. In Latin theology, a defining characteristic of a divine person. According to Thomas Aquinas there are five notions: unoriginatedness, paternity, filiation, spiration, and procession. Four of these are relations of opposition: paternity, filiation, spiration, and procession. Three relations are person-constituting: the Father is the Father of the Son, the Son is Begotten, and the Spirit is spirated. There are two processions, being begotten (the Son) and being spirated (the Spirit). There is only one God, hence only one divine essence. Below is the Latin scheme.

Unoriginat-edness	Father	Unbegotten	
Paternity	Father	Begetter of the Son	(constitutes Father as Father)
Filiation	Son	Begotten by the Father	(constitutes Son as Son)
Spiration	Father & Son	Breathe forth the Spirit	
Procession	Spirit	Breathed by Father & Son	(constitutes Spirit as Spirit)

Obediential Potency. For Rahner, the "capacity for obedience" (*potentia oboedientialis*) means the capacity of the human person to receive and respond to God's self-communication in freedom and love.

Ontic Explanation. The use of another state of affairs or set of circumstances (for example, human psychology) to explain a concept or reality (for example, the subjectivity of a person). Compare **Logical Explanation**.

Person. Greek *prosōpon* or *hypostasis*, Latin *persona* or *subsistentia*. *Prosōpon* (Latin *persona*) originally referred to the mask worn by an actor in Greek drama (cf. **hypostasis**). In christology and Trinitarian theology, "person" has had a history of diverse interpretations. Boethius (c. 480-524) defined person as "an individual substance of a rational nature"; Thomas Aquinas, as "subsisting relation." Rahner rejected the Enlightenment notion of person as individual consciousness because it failed to bring out the intrinsically relational character of person. Rahner discusses Karl Barth's definition, "mode of being," and, following Thomas, defines person as "distinct manner of subsisting."

Quasi-formal Causality. Aristotle defined four causes: material (the matter of something); efficient (that which produces something); final (the purpose of something); formal (that which makes something to be what it is, the kind of being that it is). Since divine grace cannot be a formal cause within the human person (this would make the human divine), nor is grace merely extrinsic (efficient) to the human person, Rahner qualifies formal causality with "quasi" to express that God's grace is both fully given and fully efficacious in the human person.

"Real" Relation. Constitutes something to be what it is relative to another, distinct from a *logical* relation that is an accident (for example, location or quantity). Creation has a real relation to God because without God, creation would not be at all. God, however, has a logical relation to creation because God would be God without creation.

Relation of Opposition. In Latin theology, a person is defined in terms of the person from whom the person is distinguished. For example, the Father is defined not by relation of origin (the Father comes from no one) but by relation of opposition to the Son, in relation to whom the Father is the Begetter. There are four relations of opposition: Begetting, Being Begotten, Spirating, and Being Spirated. See **Notion**.

Relation of Origin. In Greek theology, divine persons are defined "from whence they come." The Father is always Unbegotten (from no one), the Son Begotten (from the Father), the Spirit Proceeding (from the Father through, or of, the Son). See **Relations of Opposition.**

Sabellianism. A third-century form of modalism, named after Sabellius (excommunicated c. 220) who believed that God is not three distinct persons but a monad that appears in salvation history in three different ways or "modes."

Salvation History. The domain of God's self-communication, specifically, God's self-revelation and activity through Christ and the Spirit.

Self-communication (of God). God's free gift of God's self through Christ by the power of the Holy Spirit. Divine self-communication is bestowed on human beings who are created with the capacity to receive this gift. God does not give anything other than God's self, freely and completely, such that the "Gift and the Giver are one."

Spiration. Latin *spirare* (to breathe). The defining characteristic of the Holy Spirit, who, according to Latin theology, is produced by both the Father and the Son (*filioque*, "and the Son"). In

Greek theology, the Spirit proceeds from the Father "through" the Son.

Tritheism. Belief in three distinct gods.

Unbegottenness. Greek *agennēsia*, Latin *innascibilitas*. The defining property of God the Father who is without origin and "from no one," as distinct from the Son and the Spirit who originate from the Father. In Greek theology, the Father, as Unoriginate, is cause (*aitia*), font (*pēgē*), and principle (*archē*) of the Son and the Spirit. In Latin theology, in contrast, fatherhood is a property of the Father because of the Father's relationship to the Son; the Father is the Unbegotten Begetter of the Son. See **Notion**.

NOTE

The following systematic presentation presupposes several previous studies which have explained how the revelation of the Trinity was prepared and took place, and how knowledge of the mystery developed in the doctrine and practice of the Church.[1] As a consequence, our exposition will proceed through the following steps:

(1) the method and structure of the treatise *On the Triune God*[2];

(2) the main lines of the official trinitarian doctrine of the Church;

(3) a systematic outline of a theology of the Trinity.

In the third chapter we shall systematically summarize the conclusions of the two previous chapters and those of previous studies on the Trinity in the Bible and in the history of dogma. At the same time, we shall also attempt to connect the trinitarian mystery with Christian faith and life. This way of proceeding entails some repetition, since the same problem must necessarily appear against a variety of horizons.

1. See *Mysterium Salutis: Grundriss Heilsgeschichtlicher Dogmatik*, volume II, edited by Johannes Feiner and Magnus Löhrer, Einsiedeln, 1967, pp. 49ff., 85ff., 132ff., 146ff.
2. In this chapter we shall present a revised and in many ways enlarged version of our previous article, "Remarks on the Dogmatic Treatise 'De Trinitate,'" in *Theological Investigations*, volume IV, Baltimore and Dublin, 1966, pp. 77–102.

I. THE METHOD AND STRUCTURE OF THE TREATISE "ON THE TRIUNE GOD"

It is surprising that, though a considerable amount of work has been devoted to the study of the history of trinitarian theology— Petavius and de Régnon to Lebreton and Schmaus are representative of only the more illustrious names—there has been, at least until now, little momentum towards future development within this dogma. This is not to deny that religious literature has occasionally tried to situate Christian piety in more explicit and vital connection with trinitarian doctrine,[3] or that a few theologians[4]

3. We could mention, for example: V. Bernadot, *Durch die Eucharistie zur Dreifältigkeit*, Munich, 1927; E. Vandeur, "O mein Gott, Dreifaltiger, den ich anbete," in *Gebet der Schwester Elisabeth v. d. Hl. Dreifaltigkeit*, Regensburg, 1931; F. Kronseder, *Im Banne der Dreieinigkeit*, Regensburg, 1933; C. Marmion, *De H. Drieenheid in ons geestelijk leven*, Bruges, 1952; Gabriel a S. Maria Maddalena, *Geheimnis der Gottesfreundschaft*, 3 volumes, Freiburg, 1957-1958.
4. Cp. P. Laborde, *Dévotion à la Sainte Trinité*, Paris, 1922; M. Retailleau, *La Sainte Trinité dans les justes*, Paris, 1923; R. Garrigou-Lagrange, "L'habitation de la Sainte Trinité et l'expérience mystique," in *Revue thomiste* 33 (1928), pp. 449-474; M. Philipon, "La Sainte Trinité et la vie surnaturelle," in *ibid.* 44 (1938), pp. 675-698; F. Taymans d'Eypernon, *Le mystère primordial: La Trinité dans sa vivante image*, Brussels, 1946; A. Minon, "M. Blondel et le mystère de la Sainte Trinité," in *Ephemerides Theologicae Lovanienses* (Bruges) 23 (1947), pp. 472-498; J. Havet, "Mystère de la Sainte Trinité et vie chrétienne," in *Revue Dioc. Nam.* 2 (1947), pp. 161-176; F. Guimet, "Caritas ordinata et amor discretus dans la Théologie trinitaire de Richard de Saint Victor," in *Revue M. A. Lat.* 4 (1948), pp. 225-236; P. Aperribay, "Influjo causal de las divinas personas en la experiencia mística," in *Verdad y vita* 7 (1949), pp. 53-74; G. Philips, *La Sainte Trinité dans la vie du chrétien*, Liège, 1949; H. Rondet, "La Divinisation du chrétien," in *Nouvelle Revue Théologique* 71 (1949), pp. 449-476.

have become more explicitly and actively aware of their obligation to understand and present the doctrine of the Trinity in such a way that it may become a reality in the concrete life of the faithful. The textbooks of Schmaus and Philips are exemplary of this latter effort. In the history of piety, too,[5] we can see that, despite the mystical worship of the primordial, one, amodal, anonymous God, this mystery is not everywhere merely one of abstract theology, and that there is even evidence of an authentic trinitarian mysticism: thus Bonaventure, Ruysbroek, Ignatius Loyola, John of the Cross, Marie de l'Incarnation, perhaps Bérulle and a few moderns—Elizabeth of the Holy Trinity, Anton Jans.

In the theology of the Second Vatican Council the Trinity is mentioned within the context of salvation history—this being due, however, simply to the (in itself praiseworthy) "biblicism", of the conciliar statement. Such a biblicism, however, cannot by itself alone bring about a real *theological* revision of the average textbook theology of the Trinity; otherwise Scripture itself, even without being quoted in the Council, would have served as corrective.

A. The Isolation of Trinitarian Doctrine in Piety and Textbook Theology

All of these considerations should not lead us to overlook the fact that, despite their orthodox confession of the Trinity, Christians are, in their practical life, almost mere "monotheists." We must be willing to admit that, should the doctrine of the Trinity

---

5. Thus in Bonaventure, because of his exemplarism. Bonaventure attributed a great metaphysical importance to the exemplary cause, putting it on the same level as the efficient and final causes. Thus, in his own way, he overcame to a great extent the opinion that there could be no trinitarian vestiges in the world because of its creation through efficient causality by the one God.

have to be dropped as false, the major part of religious literature could well remain virtually unchanged. Nor does it help to remark that the doctrine of the *incarnation* is theologically *and* religiously so central for the Christian that, *through it,* the Trinity is always and everywhere inseparably "present" in his religious life. Nowadays when we speak of God's incarnation, the theological and religious emphasis lies only on the fact that "God" became man, that "one" of the divine persons (of the Trinity) took on the flesh, and not on the fact that this person is precisely the person of the Logos. One has the feeling that, for the catechism of head and heart (as contrasted with the printed catechism), the Christian's idea of the incarnation would not have to change at all if there were no Trinity. For God would still, as (the one) person, have become man, which is in fact about all the average Christian explicitly grasps when he confesses the incarnation. There must surely be more than one voluminous modern scientific Christology which never makes it very clear exactly *which* divine hypostasis has assumed human nature. Today's average textbook doctrine of the incarnation uses practically only the abstract concept of a divine hypostasis, despite this concept's merely analogical and precarious unity. It makes no use of the precise concept of the second divine hypostasis as such. It wishes to find out what we mean when we say that God became man, not, more specifically, what it means for the Logos, precisely as Logos, as distinct from the other divine persons, to have become man. No wonder, since starting from Augustine, and as opposed to the older tradition, it has been among theologians a more or less foregone conclusion that each of the divine persons (if God freely so decided) could have become man, so that the incarnation of precisely this person can tell us nothing about the peculiar features of *this* person within the divinity.[6]

6. There is something strange here. Every doctrine of the Trinity must emphasize that the "hypostasis" is precisely that in God through which

It is not surprising, then, that Christian piety practically re-members from the doctrine of the incarnation only that "God" has become man, without deriving from this truth any clear message about the Trinity. Thus solid faith in the incarnation does not imply that the Trinity means something in normal Christian piety. We might mention other examples which show how the present climate of piety affects dogmatic theology, despite the faint opposition deriving from the frozen hieratic formulas of ancient liturgy. Thus theology considers it almost a matter of course that the "Our Father" is addressed in the same way, with equal appositeness, indifferently to the Holy Trinity, to the three divine persons; that the sacrifice of the Mass is offered in the same manner to the three divine persons. The current doctrine of satis-faction, hence also of redemption, with its theory of a double moral subject in Christ, regards the redemptive activity as offered indifferently to the three divine persons. Such a doctrine does not give sufficient attention to the fact that satisfaction comes from the incarnate *Word*, not simply from the God-man. It supposes that another person could, as man, have offered to the triune God a *satisfactio condigna* (adequate satisfaction). It is willing to admit that such a satisfaction would be perfectly conceivable without the presupposition of the Trinity as a condition of its possibility.[7]

Father, Son, and Spirit are *distinct* from one another; that, wherever there exists between the three of them a real, univocal correspondence, there is absolute numerical identity. Hence the concept of hypostasis, applied to God, cannot be a universal univocal concept, applying to each of the three persons in the same way. Yet, in Christology, this concept is used as if it were evident that a "hypostatic function" with respect to a human nature might as well have been exercised by another hypostasis in God. Should we not at least *inquire* whether this well-determined relative sub-sistence, in which the Father and the Spirit subsist in pure distinction from—not in equality with—the Son, should not make it impossible for them (unlike in the case of the Son) to exercise such a hypostatic function with respect to a human nature. We shall take up this matter more fully on pp. 73ff., 103ff.

7. Once we presuppose the theory of a double moral person in the

Accordingly, the doctrine of grace, even if it is entitled "On the Grace of Christ," is in fact monotheistic, not trinitarian: a participation in the divine *nature* leading to a blessed vision of the divine *essence*.[8] We are told that this grace has been "merited" by Christ. But this grace of Christ is, at best, presented as the grace of the "God"-man, not as the grace of the incarnate *Word* as *Logos*. It is conceived as the recovery of a grace which, in its supralapsarian essence, is usually considered merely the grace of God, not the grace of the Word, much less of the "Word who is to become man." Thus the treatise of grace too is not much of a theological or religious introduction into the mystery of the triune God.

With notable exceptions (from Petavius to Thomassin to Scheeben and Schauf, for example) which only confirm the rule, this same anti-trinitarian timidity has induced theologians to conceive the relation brought about by grace between man and the three divine persons as one based upon "created grace," a product of God's efficient causality, merely "appropriated" differently to the single persons. The same remark applies, of course, to the treatises on the sacraments and on eschatology. Unlike the great theology of the past, as we find it in Bonaventure,[9] today's theology hardly ever sees any connection between the Trinity and the doctrine of creation. This isolation is considered legitimate, since the "outward" divine operations are "common" to the three divine per-

---

substantial unity of a person, we must admit that an absolutely one-personal God might enter into a hypostatic union with a human nature and provide satisfaction to himself.

8. In the famous constitution of Benedict XII on the beatific vision (DS 1000ff.) there is no mention of the Trinity at all. We hear only of the "divine essence," and to this essence there is attributed the most intimate personal function of *showing itself*. Can this be explained totally by the immediate context alone?

9. Cp. A. Gerken, l. c., 53ff. Also L. Scheffczyk, "Lehramtliche Formulierungen und Dogmengeschichte der Trinität," in *Mysterium Salutis*, volume II, pp. 212f.

sons, so that the world as creation cannot tell us anything about the inner life of the Trinity. The venerable classical doctrine of the "vestiges" and the "image of the Trinity" in the world is thought to be—although one would never explicitly say so—a collection of pious speculations, unobjectionable once the doctrine has been established, but telling us nothing, either about the Trinity itself or about created reality, which we did not already know from other sources.

Thus the treatise on the Trinity occupies a rather isolated position in the total dogmatic system. To put it crassly, and not without exaggeration, when the treatise is concluded, its subject is never brought up again. Its function in the whole dogmatic construction is not clearly perceived. It is as though this mystery has been revealed for its own sake, and that even after it has been made known to us, it remains, *as a reality*, locked up within itself. We make statements about it, but as a reality it has nothing to do with us at all. Average theology cannot reject all these assertions as exaggerations. In Christology it acknowledges only a hypostatic function of "one" divine person, which might as well have been exercised by any other divine person; practically it considers as important for us in Christ only that he is "one" divine person. Which divine person does not matter. It sees in divine grace only the appropriated relations of the divine persons to man, the effect of an efficient causality of the one God. In final analysis, all these statements *say explicitly* in cold print that we ourselves have nothing to do with the mystery of the Holy Trinity except to know something "about it" through revelation.[10]

10. Our objection prescinds from the fact (one that is not mentioned either in the position we attack) that real "knowledge" in its deepest metaphysical sense implies the most real conceivable relation to what is known, and the other way around. This very axiom, if thoroughly applied in our present case, would show clearly that the revelation of the mystery of the Trinity implies and presupposes ultimately a real-ontological communication to man of the revealed reality as *such*. Hence it cannot be interpreted

Someone might reply that our future happiness will consist precisely in face-to-face vision of this triune God, a vision which "introduces" us into the inner life of the divinity and constitutes our most authentic perfection, and that this is the reason why we are already told about this mystery during this life. But then we must inquire how this could be true, if between man and each one of the three divine persons there is no real ontological relation, something more than mere appropriation. How can the contemplation of any reality, even of the loftiest reality, beatify us if intrinsically it is absolutely *unrelated* to us in any way?[11] He who appeals to the beatific vision is therefore invited to draw the conclusions implied in his position. Or is our awareness of this mystery merely the knowledge of something purely extrinsic, which, as such, remains as isolated from all existential knowledge about ourselves as in our present theology the treatise on the Trinity is isolated from other dogmatic treatises telling us something about ourselves conducive to our real salvation?

B. The Problem of the Relation Between the Treatises "On the One God" and "On the Triune God"

The above remarks shed light on other facts as well, especially on the separation immemorially taken for granted between the

---

in the way which the opposed position adopts, namely, as a merely verbal communication, since this interpretation does not modify the real relation between him who communicates (*as* three-personal) and the hearer.

11. This way of formulating our position does not intend to touch the problem whether God has "real" relations *ad extra* (outwards). We may abstract from this problem here. In our context, "real-ontological," as proper to each single divine person with respect to man, should be understood only in the analogical sense (insofar as the "reality," not the specificity of the relation is concerned). Thus the Logos as such has a real relation to his human nature.

two treatises *On the One God* and *On the Triune God*, and on the sequence in which they are taught. Not a few authors have explicitly defended both as being quite essential, and theologians such as Schmaus and Stolz constitute the remarkable exception. Yet it is impossible to use tradition as a cogent argument in behalf of the usual separation and sequence of these two treatises. For they became customary only after the *Sentences* of Peter Lombard were superseded by the *Summa* of St. Thomas. If, with Scripture and the Greeks, we mean by ὁ Θεός in the first place the Father (not letting the word simply "suppose" for the Father), then the trinitarian structure of the Apostles' Creed, in line with Greek theology of the Trinity, would lead us to treat first of the Father and to consider also, in this first chapter of the doctrine of God, the "essence" of God, the Father's godhead. Thus the Master of the *Sentences* subsumed the general doctrine of God under a doctrine of the Trinity (a fact which Grabman considered one of Lombard's "main weaknesses"). Likewise in the *Summa Alexandri* there is yet no clear separation between the two treatises. As we said above, this separation took place for the first time in St. Thomas, for reasons which have not yet been fully explained. Here the first topic under study is not God the Father as the unoriginate origin of divinity and reality, but as the essence common to all three persons.[12] Such is the method

12. We are aware of the provisional nature of this statement in all its abstractness. We do not intend to anticipate the results of detailed historical investigations. Our short outline seems to be justified by the demonstrated usefulness of the transcendental-Thomistic starting point, which traditional Thomistic textbook theology has not sufficiently examined in all its possibilities and has failed to adopt. For the bearing on salvation history, see note 46. In this connection we refer the reader (for example) to the important studies of C. Sträter, S.J., who defends the following thesis concerning the starting point of the transcendental-Thomistic doctrine of the Trinity: the treatise does not start with a statement about the essence which, although common to all three persons, abstracts from the notions and the personal properties. Rather for the mature Thomas "divine essence" means the whole of the mystery of the Trinity as such. Hence

which has prevailed ever since. Thus the treatise of the Trinity locks itself in even more splendid isolation, with the ensuing danger that the religious mind finds it devoid of interest. It looks as if everything which matters for us in God has already been said in the treatise *On the One God*. This separation of the two treatises and the sequence in which they are explained probably derives from the Augustinian-Western conception of the Trinity, as contrasted with the Greek conception, even though the Augustinian conception had not, in the High Middle Ages, developed the kind of monopoly it would later enjoy. It begins with the one God, the one divine essence as a whole, and only *afterwards* does it see God as three in persons. Of course, great care is then taken and must be taken, not to set up this divine "essence" itself as a "fourth" reality pre-existing in the three persons. The Bible and the Greeks would have us start from the one unoriginate God, who is already *Father* even when nothing is known as yet about generation and spiration. He is known as the one unoriginate hypostasis which is not *positively* conceived as "absolute" even before it is explicitly known as relative.

But the medieval-Latin starting point happens to be different. And thus one may believe that Christian theology too may and should put a treatise on the one God *before* the treatise on the triune God. But since this approach is justified by the unicity of the divine essence, the only treatise which one writes, or can write, is "on the one divinity." As a result the treatise becomes quite philosophical and abstract and refers hardly at all to salva-

---

Thomas went through a conceptual development in his understanding of the divine essence, so that ultimately the difference between him and the Greek Fathers was no longer unbridgeable. This thesis stands in need of more discussion. Cp. C. Sträter, "Le point de départ du traité thomiste de *la* Trinité," *Sciences Ecclésiastiques* 14 (1962), pp. 71–87. See also, regarding this problem, K. Rahner, "Bemerkungen zur Gotteslehre in der katholischen Dogmatik," in *Catholica* 20 (1966), pp. 1–18, esp. 4–8. Regarding the relation of the treatises *On the One God* and *On the Triune God*, cp. also the literature mentioned in note 46.

tion history. It speaks of the necessary metaphysical properties of God, and not very explicitly of God as experienced in salvation history in his free relations to his creatures. For should one make use of salvation history, it would soon become apparent that one speaks always of him whom Scripture and Jesus himself calls the Father, *Jesus'* Father, who sends the Son and who gives himself to us in the Spirit, in his Spirit. On the other hand, if one starts from the basic Augustinian-Western conception, an a-trinitarian treatise "on the one God" comes as a matter of course before the treatise on the Trinity. In this event, however, the theology of the Trinity must produce the impression that it can make only purely formal statements about the three divine persons, with the help of concepts about the two processions and about the relations. Even these statements, however, refer only to a Trinity which is absolutely locked within itself—one which is not, in its reality, open to anything distinct from it; one, further, from which we are excluded, of which we happen to know something only through a strange paradox. It is true that, in an Augustinian, "psychological" theology of the Trinity efforts are made to give real content to such formal concepts[13] as procession, communica-

13. We must admit, however, that Greek theology, at its peak (with the Cappadocians), despite the fact that its doctrine of the Trinity starts in salvation history and is turned towards the world, impresses us as being even more formalistic than the theology of the Trinity in Augustine. We might perhaps explain this as follows. The Greeks thought quite naturally that the Trinity was connected with salvation history. They felt, and rightly so, that their *whole* theology was a doctrine of the Trinity. As a result, "their" doctrine of the Trinity did not investigate *everything* about the triune God, but constituted only its formal, abstract part. This part did not inquire about each one of the divine persons.

It considered only the (for them subsequent) problem of the unity of the three persons, whom they encountered as distinct both in their theology *and* in salvation history. Should we not say, then, that the West has taken over from the Greeks the formal part of the theology of the Trinity as if it were *the* (whole of) theology of the Trinity, whereas its own doctrine of salvation has kept only the dogmatically indispensable minimum of theology of the Trinity? *As a result*, unlike the Greeks, it is forced

tion of the divine essence, relation, and relative subsistence. But honesty forces us to admit that this does not lead very far. We do not mean that a psychological doctrine of the Trinity is a pure or even unsuccessful theological speculation. The hints given in Scripture show that the two divine processions, whose reality is assured by revelation, have certainly something to do with the two basic spiritual activities of knowing and loving. Thus the starting point of an Augustinian theology of the Trinity is undeniable. Yet if, unlike scholastic theology, we wish to avoid an artificial "eisegesis" into scriptural theology, we shall have to remember that this inner conception is indicated in Scripture only insofar as, in the economy of salvation, this intra-divine knowledge is seen as self-revealing, and this intra-divine love as self-communicating. When the theologian mentions this connection, as pointed out in the Scriptures, his Augustinian-psychological speculations on the Trinity result in that well-known quandary which makes all of his marvelous profundity look so utterly vacuous: for he begins from a human philosophical concept of knowledge and love, and from *this* concept develops a concept of the word and "inclination" of love; and now, after having speculatively applied these concepts to the Trinity, he must admit that this application fails, because he has clung to the "essential" concept of knowledge and love, because a "personal," "notional" concept of the word and "inclination" of love cannot be derived from human experience. For should he try so to derive it, the knowing Word and the loving Spirit themselves must in their turn have a word and a love as persons proceeding from them.[14]

---

to fill out and render more concrete such an almost mathematically formalized theology of the Trinity by means of what Augustine had developed as a "psychological" theology of the Trinity. For more details on this point, see pp. 115ff.

14. For the psychological doctrine of the Trinity and its limitations, see below, pp. 46ff., 115ff.

Things do not necessarily have to be this way every time the two treatises *On the One God* and *On the Triune God* are separated and studied in the usual sequence. Although it is certainly incorrect to claim that this separation and sequence follow the course of revelation, which would also have progressed from a revelation of the divine essence to a revelation of the three persons,[15] this separation and sequence may be considered more a didactic than a fundamental problem. The important question is: *what* is said in both treatises and how well are they related to each other, when thus separated in the usual way? What we wish to emphasize here is that, in the customary separation and sequence, the unity and the connection of the two treatises are too easily overlooked, as evidenced by the very fact that this separation and sequence are considered quite naturally as necessary and obvious.

Something else follows also from this encapsulation and isolation of the doctrine of the Trinity: the timid rejection of all attempts to discover, outside of Christendom or in the Old Testament, analogies, hints, or preparations pointing towards such a doctrine.[16] We would hardly exaggerate and oversimplify if we stated that ancient apologetics against the pagans and the Jews was mainly interested in trying to discover at least some traces of the Trinity even before the New Testament, and outside of Christendom, in a few privileged minds. The patriarchs of the Old Testament were supposed to know something about the Trinity through their faith, and the liberality with which Augustine credited the great philosophers with the knowledge of this

15. We might say at least with equal right that the history of revelation first reveals God as unoriginate person in his relation to the world, and next proceeds to the revelation of this person as the origin of intra-divine, personalizing vital processes.

16. Regarding the preparation of the revelation of the Trinity, see R. Schulte, "Die Vorbereitung der Trinitätsoffenbarung," in *Mysterium Salutis*, volume II, pp. 49–82.

mystery would scandalize us nowadays. More recent Catholic apologetics is strongly opposed to all such attempts, and no wonder, since this kind of trinitarian theology has no integral place in the world and in salvation history. When the question arises whether such vestiges can really be discovered (we should not, of course, assert *a priori* that they can), the answer is already more or less tacitly presupposed: there are no such vestiges, because there *can* not be any. At any rate, there is little desire in such attempts to attribute any positive value to trinitarian allusions or analogies in the history of religions or in the Old Testament. The *only* point which is almost always emphasized is the incommensurability of these doctrines within and outside of Christianity.

C. The Axiomatic Unity of the "Economic" and "Immanent" Trinity

The isolation of the treatise of the Trinity *has* to be wrong. There *must* be a connection between Trinity and man. The Trinity is a mystery of *salvation*, otherwise it would never have been revealed. We should show why it is such a mystery. We must point out in *every* dogmatic treatise that what it says about salvation does not make sense without referring to this primordial mystery of Christianity. Wherever this permanent perichoresis between the treatises is overlooked, we have a clear indication that either the treatise on the Trinity or the other treatises have not clearly explained connections which show how the mystery of the Trinity is for us a mystery of salvation, and why we meet it wherever our salvation is considered, even in the other dogmatic treatises.

The *basic thesis* which establishes this connection between the treatises and presents the Trinity *as* a mystery of salvation (in its reality and not merely as a doctrine) might be formulated as follows: *The "economic" Trinity is the "immanent" Trinity and the "immanent" Trinity is the "economic" Trinity.*

Of course, the correctness of this statement can, strictly speaking, be established only by what will have to be said in the third section. If we succeed at that point, with the help of this axiom, to develop systematically a doctrine of the Trinity which

first takes into account the really binding data of the doctrine of the Trinity as presented by the magisterium;

next can more naturally do justice to the biblical statements concerning the economy of salvation and its threefold structure, and to the explicit biblical statements concerning the Father, the Son, and the Spirit, so that we are no longer embarrassed by the simple fact that in reality the Scriptures do *not explicitly* present a doctrine of the "immanent" Trinity (even St. John's prologue is no such doctrine);

finally helps us to understand that in the Christian's act of faith, as *salutary* faith, and in the Christian's life the Trinity is present and has to be present;

then we shall have justified our axiom. Of course, this justification presupposes not only parts of Christology, but also some truths which must be more explicitly explained and demonstrated in the doctrine of grace—for instance, that the true and authentic concept of grace interprets grace [17] (hence also salvation history) as a *self*-communication of God (not primarily as "created grace") in Christ and in his Spirit. Grace should not be reduced to a "relation" (a purely mental relation at that) of the one God to

17. On this point see K. Rahner, "Some Implications of the Scholastic Concept of Uncreated Grace," in *Theological Investigations*, volume I, Baltimore and Dublin, 1961, pp. 319–346. *Idem*, "Gnade," in *Lexikon für Theologie und Kirche*, volume IV, Freiburg, 1960, pp. 991–1000; "Selbstmitteilung Gottes," in *ibid*. (1959), p. 627; L. Willig, "Geschaffene und ungeschaffene Gnade," in *Münsterische Beiträge zur Theologie* 27 (Münster, 1964).

the elected creature, nor to a relation which is merely "appropriated" to the other divine persons. In the recipient himself grace is not some created sanctifying "quality" produced in a merely causal way by the one God. All this is presupposed. Yet in order to justify the basic axiom of our doctrine of the Trinity, we must at once propose a few remarks about it.

The "economic" Trinity *is* the immanent Trinity, according to the statement which interests us. In one way this statement is a defined doctrine of the faith.[18] Jesus is not simply God in general, but the Son. The second divine person, God's Logos, is man, and only he is man. Hence there is at least *one* "mission," *one* presence in the world, *one* reality of salvation history which is not merely appropriated to some divine person, but which is proper to him. Here we are not merely *speaking* "about" this person in the world. Here something occurs "outside" the intra-divine life in the world itself, something which is not a mere effect of the efficient causality of the triune God acting as one in the world, but something which belongs to the Logos alone, which is the history of one divine person, in contrast to the other divine persons. This remains true even if we admit that this hypostatic union which belongs exclusively to the Logos is causally effected by the whole Trinity. There has occurred in salvation history something which can be predicated only of one divine person. At any rate, this *one* case shows up as *false* the statement that there is nothing in salvation history, in the economy of salvation, which cannot equally be said of the triune God as a whole and of each person in particular. On the other hand, the following statement too is *false*: that a doctrine of the Trinity treating of the divine persons in general and of each person in particular can speak only of that which occurs within the divinity itself. And we are sure

18. To be sure, first *only* for one point, in one instance. This does not suffice by itself to justify our thesis as a whole, as plainly a doctrine of faith.

that the following statement is true: that no adequate distinction can be made between the doctrine of the Trinity and the doctrine of the economy of salvation.[19]

D. The Incarnation as an "Instance" of a More Comprehensive Reality

The bearing of the above considerations upon our problem is often weakened or obscured in theology by three lines of thought. We must, therefore, first examine them before we can expose the importance of the dogmatically certain starting point of our wider thesis.

I. THE SPECIAL NATURE OF THE "HYPOSTATIC" UNION

The *first difficulty*, which is also the best known, the most comprehensive, and the most radical, is the following: When one appeals to the hypostatic union, he builds his case upon a dogmatically certain reality. Yet he is wrong, because this is not and *cannot* be an instance or an example of a general situation or principle. We should not even envisage the possibility of taking the statement about the hypostatic union as a paradigm for

19. There is no getting away from this statement by the crafty textbook objection that the hypostatic union does not bring about a "real relation" in the Logos himself, hence that nothing referring to salvation history must be stated of the Logos as such which concerns him. We shall not discuss here the axiom of scholastic metaphysics which claims that God has no "real relations" to the world. One thing is certain and should serve as guiding *norm* for this axiom (and not the other way around!): the Logos himself is truly man, he himself, only he, and not the Father and not the Spirit. Hence it remains true forever that, if in a doctrine of the divine persons we have to say of the Logos himself all that which is and remains real in him, this doctrine implies itself an "economic" statement. For more details about this objection, see K. Rahner, "On the Theology of the Incarnation," in *Theological Investigations*, volume IV, pp. 105-120, esp. pp. 112ff.

similar statements which would likewise open the Trinity towards the world, and thus lead to the thesis of an identity between the economic and the immanent Trinity. The reason we cannot consider the incarnation as an "instance" of a wider state of affairs is simple and peremptory. In God everything is identically one whenever we are not speaking of the opposition of the relations of origin which gives rise to the three persons.[20] Consequently it is only through a *hypostatic* union as such that a single divine person, as distinct from the other divine persons, can have his own proper relation to the world. For only in such a union is there actualized what is proper to the person, the personality, the "outward" hypostatic function. Now there is only one hypostatic union, that of the Logos; moreover, every *proper* relation of each person can be only hypostatic. It follows that from the truth of the incarnation no general principle can be derived except that it is possible for other divine persons also to enter into a hypostatic union.

It is not our task or purpose to enter into this basic difficulty, as presented during the last decades mainly by Paul Galtier[21] against all claims that grace gives rise to not-appropriated relations of divine persons to man. This theme has been so thoroughly treated that, within the framework of these short introductory remarks, we can say nothing better or more about it. Hence it is enough to note that the refutation of the objection, as presented, for instance, by H. Schauf,[22] seems to be conclusive. The least we

20. Cp. for the history, the meaning, and the limits of this principle the rich study of H. Mühlen, "Person und Appropriation: Zum Verständnis des Axioms: In Deo omnia sunt unum, ubi non obviat relationis oppositio," in *Münchener theologische Studien* 16 (1965), pp. 37–57.

21. P. Galtier, *L'habitation en nous des trois personnes*, Rome, 1952.

22. H. Schauf, *Die Einwohnung des Heiligen Geistes*, Freiburg, 1941; cp. also P. J. Donnelly, "The Inhabitation of the Holy Spirit: A Solution According to de la Taille," in *Theological Studies* 8 (1947), pp. 445–470; J. Trütsch, *SS. Trinitatis inhabitatio apud theologos recentiores*, Trent, 1949; S. J. Dockx, *Fils de Dieu par grâce*, Paris, 1948; C. Sträter, "Het

25

can say is that Galtier and other theologians who share his opinion
have not clearly established that a hypostatically special relation
and a hypostatic unitive relation are necessarily and strictly the
same thing. Later we shall meet positive arguments against this
identification.[23]

Yet we may add a few remarks of our own against Galtier.
First, he and his followers take it too much for granted that we
know clearly and distinctly what is meant by "person" and
"hypostasis" when these concepts are applied to God's "threefoldness" and to Christ, and that "person" as used in Christology

---

begrip 'appropriate' bij S. Thomas," in *Bijdragen* 9 (1948), pp. 1-41, 144-
186; J. H. Nicolas, "Présence trinitaire et présence de la Trinité," in
Revue Thomiste 50 (1950), pp. 183-191; Th. J. Fitzgerald, *De inhabitatione
Spiritus Sancti in doctrina S. Thomae Aquinatis*, Mundelein, 1950; P. De
Letter, "Sanctifying Grace and Our Union with the Holy Trinity," in
Theological Studies 13 (1952), pp. 33-58; P. Donnelly, "Sanctifying Grace
and Our Union with the Holy Trinity: A Reply," in *ibid.* 13 (1952),
pp. 190-204; F. Bourassa, "Adoptive Sonship: Our Union with the Divine
Persons," in *ibid.*, pp. 309-335; P. De Letter, "Current Theology: Sanctify-
ing Grace and the Divine Indwelling," in *ibid.* 14 (1953), pp. 242-272;
E. Bourassa, "Présence de Dieu et Union aux divines personnes," in
Sciences Ecclésiastiques 6 (1954), pp. 3-23; *idem*, "Divine Indwelling and
Sanctifying Grace," *Bijdragen* 19 (1958), pp. 22-31; E. Haible, "Die Einwohnung der drei göttlichen Personen im Christen nach den Ergebnissen
der neueren Theologie," in *Theologische Quartalschrift* 139 (1959), pp. 1-
27; H. Mühlen, *Der Heilige Geist als Person*, Münster, 1963; I. Willig,
Geschaffene und ungeschaffene Gnade, pp. 260ff., 283ff. (Lit.); M. Flick
and Z. Alszeghy, *Il Vangelo della Grazia*, Firenze 1964, pp. 454-498
(abundant literature).

23. Attention is drawn upon the method we use. First the argument is
purely *negative*: we say that the reasons given by Galtier, for example, are
not peremptory. Hence we do not say *positively* that from the *sole* fact of
the incarnation as such we may *infer* that there might still be other instances of such a real involvement of the immanent Trinity in the world.
Otherwise we would contradict ourselves. For we shall have to say very
soon that we may not conclude from the incarnation of the Logos to the
possibility of the incarnation of another divine person. It is only by
mentioning theological reasons for the opinion that there are other
instances of such a correspondence of economic and immanent Trinity that
we can show how the incarnation may be considered an "instance" of such
an identity.

means *simply* the same thing as in the Trinity.[24] More attention should be paid to the different *origin* of these two concepts of person (person as that which distinguishes—person as a principle of unity, each with respect to one or two natures), especially since "hypostasis" and "hypostatic function" can only be verbally distinguished in the incarnation. With this in mind we may at least *inquire*: might it not derive from the peculiar nature of the second person (and respectively from that of the third person) that, when the one God communicates himself to the world, the peculiarity of this self-communication, insofar as it is determined by the peculiarity of the second person, consists in becoming a "hypostatic union," whereas such would not be the case if this self-communication were determined by the peculiarity of the third person? Yet the third person too might be capable of self-communication, and assume a not-appropriated relation to the creature. In brief, if it is not certain that "hypostatic" in the union of the Logos with created reality is to be understood *only* from the concept of "one" hypostasis of the Trinity, if it rather derived its content from the proper nature precisely of the Logos as such, then the presupposition tacitly made by Galtier and others in their demonstration no longer looks so certain.

Hence we assert that, in principle, the incarnation may be considered as a dogmatically certain "instance" for a (theoretically at least not impossible) economic relation, proper to each person, of the divine persons to the world. Such a relation entails the possibility of a real communication, in salvation history, of the whole Trinity as such to the world, therefore the identity of the economic and the immanent Trinity. This is especially true since such a conception does *not* imply that these three not-appropriated relations of the three persons to the world stand

24. We shall take up this problem in more detail in our third chapter.

independently near each other. It may very well mean that the threefold God *as* threefold possesses in his divine self-communication "one" relationship to creation, but precisely a relationship which refers him *as* threefold, each person in his own way, to the world.

2. THE INCARNATION OF THE LOGOS AND THE IMMANENT TRINITY

The *second,* in a way opposite, difficulty has already been hinted at. If we admit that *every* divine person might assume a hypostatic union with a created reality, then the fact of the incarnation of the Logos "reveals" properly nothing about the Logos *himself,* that is, about his own relative specific features within the divinity. For in this event the incarnation means for us practically only the experience that God in general is a person, something which we already knew. It does not mean that in the Trinity there is a very special differentiation of persons. Although we *know* (having been told so in statements) that precisely the *second* divine person exercises a hypostatic function with respect to the human reality visible in Jesus, there would be no difference in our experience if some other divine person constituted the subsistence of this human reality. Since Jesus speaks of the Father and of himself as "Son," the reality which we perceive in salvation history yields us an outlook into the Trinity through words, not through itself. Since that which *happens* in salvation history might have happened through each other person, since it is but the neutral vehicle of a merely verbal revelation, not the revelation of some intra-trinitarian occurrence, it tells us nothing about intra-trinitarian life.

We have indicated above how this taken-for-granted presupposition influences the development of Christology. Is this presupposition true, is it true that *every* divine person might become man? We answer that it is not demonstrated and that it is false.

It is not demonstrated. The most ancient tradition, before Augustine, has never considered such a possibility and has at bottom always presupposed the opposite in its theological considerations. For the Father is by definition the Unoriginate, the one who is in principle "invisible," who reveals himself and appears precisely by sending his *Word* into the world. The Word is, by definition, immanent in the divinity *and* active in the world, and as such the Father's revelation. A revelation of the Father without the Logos and his incarnation would be like speaking without words.

The presupposition is false. From the mere fact that one divine person has become man, the same "possibility" cannot be deduced for another person. Such a deduction would presuppose two things:

(a) that "hypostasis" is in God a univocal concept with respect to the three divine persons;

(b) that the different ways in which each person is a person would not prevent a person, precisely through that which makes him a unique person, from entering into a hypostatic relation with a created reality, like the second divine person. (We should keep in mind that the ways in which each person is a person are so different that they allow of only a *very loosely* analogical concept of person, as *equally* applicable to the three persons.) Now of these two presuppositions the former is false and the latter is by no ways demonstrated.[25]

25. He who denies that the Father or the Spirit too might have become man would deny them a "perfection" only if it had first been established that such a possibility is a real possibility, *hence* a "perfection" for the Father or for the Spirit. But precisely this is not sure. Thus it is, for instance, a perfection for the *Son* as Son to descend from the Father. But it would be pure nonsense to conclude thence that the Father as such should also possess this perfection. Since the hypostatic function "outwards" *is* the corresponding divine hypostasis, we are not allowed to deduce anything for another hypostasis from the function of *this* hypostasis,

The rejected thesis is false. Should it be true, and not merely mentioned at the fringe of theological thinking, but really presented in earnest,[26] it would create havoc with theology. There would no longer be any connection between "mission" and the intra-trinitarian life. Our sonship in grace would in fact have absolutely nothing to do with the Son's sonship, since it might equally well be brought about without any modification by another incarnate person. That which God is for us would tell us absolutely nothing about that which he is in himself, as triune. These and many similar conclusions, which would follow from this thesis, go against the whole sense of holy Scripture. This will be denied only by him who does not put his theology under the norm of Scripture, but allows the latter to tell him only that which he knows already from his textbook theology, cleverly and ruthlessly distinguishing all the rest away. This should and could be shown in detail. Here, however, we can only establish the opposite thesis. Since the thesis which we reject can claim no dogmatic or theological authority for itself, we may within the context of these brief preparatory remarks simply state that we reject it. In this way we stay more faithfully than the rejected opinion within the framework of that which has truly been revealed. We develop a theology which neither explicitly nor (more dangerously) implicitly considers a pretended possibility never mentioned in revelation; we cling to the truth that the Logos is really as he appears in revelation, that he is *the one* who reveals to us (not merely *one* of those who might have revealed to us) the triune God, on account of the personal being which belongs exclusively to him, the Father's Logos.

even when our *abstract* universal concept of subsistence shows no contradiction with the hypothesis that the Father should cause a human nature to subsist.

26. We have already shown at the beginning of this chapter how this thesis, although almost tacitly taken for granted, has considerable influence and is therefore anonymously quite powerful.

3. THE IDENTITY OF THE "ECONOMIC" AND "IMMANENT" LOGOS

The *third* difficulty against our basic axiom,[27] one which alone brings out the full strength of the second objection, is the following: Suppose we interpret the human nature of the Logos *only* as something which rests in itself, in its separate essence, as something created after a plan or an "idea" which in itself has nothing to do with the Logos, or at any rate not more than other possible natures or essences. Then this nature subsists in the Logos, and we may predicate this natural reality and its activities of the Logos as his own. We may in a formal, but only in a very formal sense, say that through this human reality the Logos is "present" and "active" in the world and its history. But this whole reality "conveys" to us nothing about the Logos as such. Here the Logos shows us only the universal, that which is "human" also outside of him. At most he shows us, *through* this reality, marvelous and superhuman features: the preternatural gifts, which belong to no other human nature, but which we observe in him. But the human as such would not show us

27. As a rule this difficulty occurs in theology only anonymously. It is difficult even to formulate it clearly, although it probably lies in the background of all christological differences persisting even today in Catholic Christology—for instance, between a pure Chalcedonism and a neo-Chalcedonism. The question is this: is the humanity of the Logos merely something foreign which has been assumed, or is it precisely that which comes into being when the Logos ex-presses himself into the non-divine? Should we start from human nature as from something we already know, as something not more clearly revealed by the incarnation, when we try to explain this incarnation in its real content (with respect to that which the Logos becomes)? Or should human nature *ultimately* be explained through the self-emptying self-utterance of the Logos himself? On this problem and the following questions see K. Rahner, "Current Problems in Christology," in *Theological Investigations*, volume I, pp. 149–200; "On the Theology of the Incarnation," in *Theological Investigations*, volume IV, pp. 105–120; B. Welte, *Zur Christologie von Chalkedon: Auf der Spur des Ewigen*, Freiburg, 1965, pp. 429–458.

the Logos as such. Here too he would show himself only in his formal subjectivity. And we would have to admit that an intra-divine trinitarian reality has proceeded outwards into true salvation history only in a purely formal way. That which is already known to us, that which is not trinitarian, is created; *as such*, as already presupposed (logically, ontologically, not temporally presupposed), it is assumed. But in this hypothesis we cannot say that the Logos has stepped outside his intra-divine inaccessibility and shown *himself through* his humanity and *in* his humanity. In this same hypothesis we could not really say: He who *sees* me, sees *me*. For, when we glimpse the humanity of Christ as such, we would in reality have seen nothing of the subject of the Logos himself, except at most his abstract formal subjectivity.

Hence the question is: Shall we interpret the Chalcedonian ἀσυγχύτως in such a way that the unblended human nature of the Logos has to the Logos as Logos no other relation than that of any creature whatsoever to its creator, except for a formal subsisting within him? Thus this nature would be "said" of its subject, but this subject would not "express" *itself* in it. Perhaps we have not even succeeded in lifting the difficulty itself into the light of reflex awareness. Yet it lies dimly at the basis of every Christology, and its very dimness renders it even more active and more disturbing.

It is even less possible really to establish the answer which we consider the correct one to this question. Suffice it to say: No, we do not accept the way in which the difficulty mentioned above sees the basic relationship between the Logos and the assumed human nature in Christ. The relation which exists between the two is more essential and more intimate. Human nature in general is a possible object of the creative knowledge and power of God, because and insofar as the Logos is by nature the one who is "utterable" (even into that which is not God); because he is the Father's Word, in which the Father can express himself, and, freely, empty himself into the non-divine; because, when this happens, that precisely is born which we call human nature. In other words, human nature is not a mask (the πρόσωπον) assumed from without, from behind which the Logos hides to act things out in the world. From the start it is the constitutive, real symbol of the Logos himself.[28] So that we may and should say, when we think our ontology through to the end: man is possible because the exteriorization of the Logos is possible. We cannot expose this thesis here in more detail, even less can we demonstrate it. Rather we refer the reader to recent publications[29] which treat of this problem explicitly or by indirection. And if our question should be answered in the indicated way, we may say without weakening our assertion, or secretly taking back part of it that: what Jesus is and does as man reveals the Logos himself; it is the reality of the Logos as our salvation amidst us. Then we can assert, in the full meaning of the words: here the Logos with God and the Logos with us, the immanent and the economic Logos, are strictly the same.[30]

28. On this concept cp. my paper "The Theology of the Symbol," in *Theological Investigations*, volume IV, pp. 221–252.

29. Cp. the literature mentioned in notes 27 and 28. Also F. Malmberg, *Der Gottmensch*, Freiburg, 1959.

30. Since our problem concerns not the formal subject of the Logos in the abstract, but the concrete incarnate Logos, this sameness is the one about which Ephesus and Chalcedon both say that it is unconfused, unseparated, hence not the sameness of a lifeless identity in which there is nothing to distinguish because from the start everything is identically the same, but the sameness in which one and the same Logos is *himself* in the human reality not because something foreign (human nature) has been joined to him in a merely additive way, but because the Logos posits this other reality as his way of positing and expressing himself. In the case of mere addition this "joining" could no longer be thought as a real one. We would simply have a case where two realities are thought of as *juxtaposed*. In fact, the difference should be conceived as an inner modality of the unity. Thus within the Trinity and "outside" it an immediate sameness not mediated by something really different should be considered not as the highest form, but rather as a negation of authentic sameness.

E. God's Threefold Relation to Us in the Order of Grace

The economic Trinity *is* the immanent Trinity—such is the statement which we have to explain. We have shown above that there is at least *one* instance of this axiom which is dogmatically above doubt. That this instance is really an *instance* becomes clear only when we reflect on the doctrine of grace. The instance in question is that of the not-appropriated relations of the divine persons to the justified. Since we have already indicated the problem and the differences of opinion among theologians concerning it, we shall not have to mention them again. At any rate, the least we may say is that this thesis of the proper, not-appropriated relations is a free and unobjectionable opinion in theology. We presuppose it here.[31] Our only task will be to develop this well-known, current, albeit not unquestioned doctrine in the light of our problem. When correctly understood and taken seriously, the thesis which we presuppose here as true[32] states not some scholastic subtlety, but simply this: each one of the three divine persons communicates himself to man in gratuitous grace in his own

31. We draw attention to one point. If we apply the classical ontology and theology of the beatific vision to the undeniable intuition of the divine persons as such, we cannot logically reject this thesis for the vision nor for justifying grace as the ontological substratum and formal beginning of the immediate intuition of God. An immediate intuition of the divine persons, not mediated by a created "impressed species" but only by the ontological reality of the intuited object in itself (which gives itself in a real quasi-formal causality to the intuiting subject as the ontological condition of the possibility of the formal knowledge) means necessarily an ontological relation of the intuiting subject to each one of the intuited persons as such in their real particularity. Medieval theology may not have given enough thought to this consideration, although it lies altogether in the line of its theological approach to the vision.

32. This will be further corroborated, although only by means of a few hints, pp. 76f., when we shall briefly examine the factual history of the revelation of the Trinity.

personal particularity and diversity. This trinitarian communication is the ontological ground of man's life of grace and eventually of the direct vision of the divine persons in eternity. It is God's "indwelling," "uncreated grace," understood not only as a communication of the divine nature, but also and primarily, since it implies a free personal act, since it occurs from person to person, as a communication of "persons." Of course, this self-communication of the persons occurs according to their personal peculiarity, that is, also according to and in virtue of their mutual relations. Should a divine person communicate himself otherwise than in and through his relations to the other persons, so as to have his own relation to the justified (and the other way around), this would presuppose that each single divine person, even as such, as mentally distinct from the one and same essence, would be something absolute and not merely relative. We would no longer be speaking of the Trinity. In other words: these three self-communications are the self-communication of the one God in the three relative ways in which God subsists. The Father gives himself to us too as *Father*, that is, precisely because and insofar as he himself, being essentially with *himself*, utters himself and *in this way* communicates the Son as his own, personal self-manifestation;[33] and because and insofar as the Father and the Son (receiving from the Father), welcoming each other in love, drawn and returning to each other, communicate themselves *in this way*, as received in mutual love, that is, as Holy Spirit. God relates to us in a threefold manner, and this threefold, free, and gratuitous relation to us *is* not merely a copy or an analogy of the inner Trinity, but this Trinity itself, albeit as freely and gratuitously communicated. That which is communicated is precisely the

---

33. We cannot yet explain in more detail that and how the self-communication of the Father in the uttering of the Word in the world means for the believer both incarnation and the promise *in grace* of this Word. They imply each other.

triune personal God, and likewise the communication bestowed upon the creature in gratuitous grace can, *if* occurring in freedom, occur only in the intra-divine manner of the two communications of the divine essence by the Father to the Son and the Spirit. Any other kind of communication would be unable to communicate that which is here communicated, the divine persons, since these persons do not differ from their own way of communicating themselves.

Anticipating somewhat our later exposition (because there is no other way of explaining the "method" we are using), we may now consider from the other direction the connection between immanent and economic Trinity. The one God communicates himself in absolute self-utterance and as absolute donation of love. Here is the absolute mystery revealed to us only by Christ: God's self-communication is truly a *self*-communication. He does not merely indirectly give his creature some share of himself *by* creating and giving us created and finite realities through his omnipotent *efficient* causality. In a *quasi-formal* causality he really and in the strictest sense of the word bestows *himself*.[34] Now the testimony of revelation in Scripture tells us that this self-communication of God has a threefold aspect.[35] It is the self-

34. It follows as a formal axiom that if the distinction present in something communicated by God exists *only* on the creature's side, then there is no *self*-communication of God in the strict sense. If, on the other hand, there is a real *self*-communication with a real distinction in that which is communicated as such, hence with a real distinction "for us," then God must "in himself" carry this distinction. His unity is not affected, and we characterize it as the unity of the absolute "essence." The distinction is also characterized as a relative manner of being related to himself. Hence we may say that if revelation (a) testifies to a real *self*-communication, and (b) explains this self-communication as containing distinctions "for us," that is considers it as mediated, of a mediation that is not merely created (which would do away with the character of a real self-communication), then it affirms *ipso facto* distinction and mediation in God as he is in himself.

35. What follows will be explained in greater detail in our third chapter. The purpose of our present remarks is only to clarify the basic axiom as such.

communication[36] in which that which is given remains sovereign, incomprehensible, continuing, even as received, to dwell in its uncontrollable incomprehensible originality. It is a self-communication in which the God who manifests himself "is there"[37] as self-uttered truth and as freely, historically disposing sovereignty. It is a self-communication, in which the God who communicates himself causes in the one who receives him the act of loving welcome, and causes it in such a way that his welcoming does not bring the communication down to the purely created level.

We must avoid two misunderstandings. On the one hand, this threefold aspect of the self-communication should not, in the dimension of communication, be interpreted as a merely *verbal* unfolding of a communication which in itself contains no distinctions. In the dimension of salvation history, this distinction is truly "real." The origin of God's self-communication, its "existence" as it radically expresses and utters itself, the self-communication's welcoming acceptance brought about by himself, are not indistinctly "the same thing" signified by different words. That is: as understood by the experience of faith, based on the witness of Scripture, the Father, the Word, and the Spirit (however deficient all these words may and must be) point to a true distinction, to a double mediation within this self-communication. On the other hand, the history of this self-communication, as it reveals itself, has shown ever more closely and more undeniably that this double mediation by Word and Spirit is not a created kind of mediation, in which God would not really be communicated as he is in himself. The testimony of faith tells

36. Concerning this concept cp. the literature mentioned in note 17.

37. We must bear in mind that the concept of "Word" should be interpreted with all the fullness of the meaning in the Old Testament, hence as the powerful creative Word of God that acts and decides, in which the Father ex-presses himself, in which he is present and active. We have never to do with a mere theoretical self-reflection. Such a concept makes it much easier for us to understand the unity of the "Word" of God as incarnate and as powerfully directing and disposing in the heart of man.

that the economic self-communication of God is truly and really threefold.[38] *Economic* Sabellianism is false. The mediations of God among us are no created intermediaries or world powers. Such a conception of God's communication would basically be Arian, it would do away with a true *self*-communication of God, it would bring down the eschatological salvific work of Christ to the level of forever provisory and open mediations, after the manner of prophetic-servants, of angelic powers, or of gnostic-neo-Platonic descending emanations. It follows that this real mediation of a divine kind in the dimension of salvation history must also *be* a real mediation in God's inner life. The "threefoldness" of God's relation to us in Christ's order of grace is already the reality of God as it is in itself: a three-personal one. This statement would constitute Sabellianism or modalism only if the following conditions were fulfilled: if it totally ignored the fact that this modality is one of radical *self*-manifestation in uncreated grace and in the hypostatic union; if it claimed that God himself is so little affected by this relation that this "diversity" would, as in creation and in God's natural relation to the world, bring about no difference in God, only a difference in his creatures.

F. *The Methodological Importance of Our Basic Thesis*

How is the method of our systematic explanation of the doctrine of the Trinity affected when the thesis that the economic Trinity is the immanent Trinity and the immanent Trinity is the economic Trinity is presupposed (or eventually confirmed)?

---

38. Cp. what F. J. Schierse writes about the revelation of the Trinity in the New Testament, in *Mysterium Salutis*, volume II, pp. 87ff., 97ff., 113ff., 125ff.

I. THE TRINITY AS A SALVIFIC EXPERIENCE
AND AN EXPERIENCE OF GRACE

First, we may in this treatise confidently look for an access into the doctrine of the Trinity in Jesus and in his Spirit, as we experience them through faith in salvation history. For in these two persons the immanent Trinity itself *is* already given. The Trinity is not for us a reality which can only be expressed as a doctrine. The Trinity itself is with us, it is not merely given to us because revelation offers us statements about it. Rather these statements are made to us because the reality of which they speak is bestowed upon *us*. They are not made in order to test our faith in something to which we have no real relation. They are made because the grace we have received and the glory we expect cannot wholly become manifest if we are not told about this mystery. Thus the two mysteries, that of our grace and that of God in himself, constitutes one and the same abysmal mystery. The treatise on the Trinity should always keep this in mind. It is thence, from this most existential concern for our salvation, that it lives, that it receives its impulsion, that it becomes really comprehensible. For him who rejects our basic thesis the Trinity can *only* be something which, as long as we do not contemplate it immediately in its absolute "in itself,"[39] can be told about in purely conceptual statements, through a merely *verbal* revelation, as opposed to God's *salvific activity* in us. Then, however, the treatise takes on the abstract impractical character which is so frequent in such systems. Then the proof from Scripture will unavoidably begin to look like a method which, by the use of subtle dialectical tricks, tries to draw conclusions from a few scattered statements, putting them together in a system about which we cannot help

39. Provided that an intuition understood *in this sense* implies or seems to imply no inner contradiction.

wondering whether God has really revealed to us such abstruse things in a manner which is so obscure and needs so many complicated explanations. But if it is true that we can really grasp the content of the doctrine of the Trinity only by going back to the history of salvation and of grace, to our experience of Jesus and of the Spirit of God, who operates in us, because in them we really already possess the Trinity itself as such, then there never should be a treatise on the Trinity in which the doctrine of the "missions" is at best only appended as a relatively unimportant and additional scholion. Every such treatise should from its very start be animated by this doctrine, even when, for didactic reasons, it is treated explicitly only at the end of the treatise of the Trinity, or even in other sections of dogmatic theology.[40] We might even say that the less a doctrine of the Trinity fears treating its topic from the point of view of salvation history, the more chance there is that it will say all that which matters about the immanent Trinity, and that it will say it in such a way that a theoretical and existential understanding of the faith may really grasp it.

2. ON INTERPRETING THE HISTORY
OF TRINITARIAN REVELATION

If we follow the method recommended above, the treatise may (whether explicitly or implicitly is a purely didactic and secondary problem) follow the same order as the history of the revelation of this mystery. Our modern theology is wont to reject too simply, apodictically, and unreservedly the opinion of the ancients that, even before Christ, there was already in some vague way a

40. F. Bourassa shows in his article "Sur le traité de la Trinité," in *Gregorianum* 47 (1966), pp. 254–285, esp. 277ff. (on the "missions"), how difficult it is to combine the salvation history approach and the speculative approach, if one adheres to the traditional starting point.

belief in the Trinity. Our point of view might help the treatise on the Trinity introduce a few more nuances in the evaluation of this position. It would allow us to understand better the opinion of the ancients and the history of the revelation of this mystery.[41]

Throughout the Old Testament there runs the basic theme that God is the absolute mystery, whom nobody can see without dying, and that it is nevertheless this God *himself* who conversed with the Fathers through his actions in history. This revealing self-manifestation is, in the Old Testament, mediated mostly (not to mention Yahweh's Angel, etc.) by the "Word," which, while causing God to be present in power, also represents him; and by the "Spirit," who helps men to understand and to announce the Word.[42] When these two are not active, Yahweh has retreated from his people. When he bestows upon the "holy remnant" his renewed and forever victorious mercy, he sends *the* prophet with his Word in the fullness of the Spirit. (The Torah and Wisdom doctrine of sapiential literature is only a more individualistic version of the same basic conception. It pays less attention to historical development.) God is present in the unity of Word and Spirit.

In a certain sense, theoretically no great distance separates these three realities. His presence through the Word in the Spirit must be different from him, the lasting primordial mystery, yet it cannot stand before him and hide him as if it were something quite different. Hence when we reach the point of absolute *proximity* of the "coming" of God, the covenant, in which God really communicates himself radically and bindingly to his partner, then the whole development of this history allows of only two possibilities. Either God's Word and his Spirit disappear as

41. Especially for the real history of the *concepts* which, in an historical development, have slowly and legitimately acquired their trinitarian meaning.

42. Cp. the chapter by R. Schulte in *Mysterium Salutis*, volume II, pp. 63ff.

(mere) *created* mediations, as the many prophets with their many words disappeared before the supreme and overpowering personal presence of God, which appears now as the secret goal of God's partnership at all times. Or these two "mediations" persist, revealing themselves as truly divine, hence as God himself, in unity with, yet distinct from the God of revelation, in a unity and a distinction which belong therefore to God himself. In this sense we must admit an authentic secret prehistory of the revelation of the Trinity in the Old Testament. This prehistory, which, after all, nobody can wholly deny, removes the impression that certain concepts, with their long history, have been applied to an utterance of the New Testament (and even more of the later doctrine of the Church), with which, considered in themselves, they had *absolutely nothing* in common.

3. ON HIDDEN MISUNDERSTANDINGS AND PROBLEMS OF TERMINOLOGY

Such an insistence upon the unity of the immanent and economic doctrine of the Trinity might also remove a danger which, however one may feel about it, has remained the real danger in the doctrine of the Trinity, not so much in the abstract theology of the textbooks, but in the average conception of the normal Christian. This is the danger of a popular, unverbalized, but at bottom quite massive tritheism.[43] Whenever efforts are made to

43. We must continually avoid the following dilemma: either we find in religious consciousness, as mentioned above, an absence of the Trinity, and nothing but a rigid, unmediated sheer monotheism; or, when efforts are made to realize the truth of the Trinity, there arises in religious consciousness a tritheism which is overcome only verbally by the (never denied) confession of God's unity. What is lacking is the awareness of a mediating principle which would allow us to conceive of the inner *unity* and unicity and trinity in God, not only in formal static abstractness, or for "God in himself," but also concretely and for us, that is, in some reality which may always be concretely realized in ourselves, in the mystery,

think of the Trinity, this danger looms much larger than that of Sabellian modalism. There can be no doubt about it: speaking of three persons in God entails almost inevitably the danger (as a rule we try much too late to overcome it through explicit corrections) of believing that there exist in God three distinct consciousnesses, spiritual vitalities, centers of activity, and so on. This danger is increased by the fact that, even in the usual presentation of the scholarly treatises on the Trinity, there is *first* developed a concept of "person" derived from experience and philosophy, independently of the doctrine of the Trinity as found in revelation and of the history of this doctrine. Next this concept is applied to God, and thus it is demonstrated that there are three *such* persons in God. Further in the usual treatise, when the relation between unicity and triple personality in God is being considered, the necessary explanations are given as to how we should correctly interpret these three "persons" in God. Thus it is rather implicitly and belatedly that the required modifications and distinctions are made in the concept of person with which we set out on our spiritual odyssey upon the sea of God's mystery. But honesty finally forces us to inquire, not without misgivings, why we still call "persons" that which remains ultimately of God's threefold "personality," since we have to remove from these persons precisely that which at first we thought of as constituting a person. Later on, when the more subtle remarks of the theologians have been forgotten, we see that once more we glide probably into a false and basically tritheistic conception, as we think of the three persons as of three different personalities with different centers of activity. We wonder why we did not from the start operate with a concept or word ("person" or some other word) which might more easily be adapted to that which is meant

which gives itself to us through the Word in the Spirit, and as Word and Spirit.

and express it with less danger of misunderstanding. We do not agree with Karl Barth that the word "person" is ill adapted to express the intended reality and that it should be replaced in ecclesiastical terminology by another word which produces fewer misunderstandings. Yet we must grant that the later development of the word "person" outside of the doctrine of the Trinity after the formulation of the dogma in the fourth century has further increased its ambiguity.[44] From the original almost Sabellian meaning it has evolved to the existential and Hermesian meaning of an "Ego" opposed to every other person in autonomous and distinct freedom. Yet the word "person" happens to be there, it has been consecrated by the use of more than 1500 years, and there is no really better word, which can be understood by all and would give rise to fewer misunderstandings. So we shall have to keep it, although we must keep its history in mind and realize that, absolutely speaking, it is not in every respect well adapted to express what is meant and that it does not lack certain disadvantages. But if we use the economic approach to the mystery of the Trinity clearly and systematically, we are not obliged, any more than the history of revelation itself, to begin this treatise with the concept of "person."[45] We may start from the self-revelation of God (the Father) as given in salvation history, as mediated by the Word in the Spirit. We may show that these distinctions of "God for us" are also those of "God in himself." Next we simply explain that this reality which is threefold in

44. In the third chapter we shall speak in more detail about this basic difficulty.

45. The fact that the concept of person has been approved by Church law in this connection should not necessarily and always mean that it must be the *starting* point of *every* theological study. It may also be the end point which we reach by following in our theological thinking the same order that was followed in the development of revelation and of *Church* doctrine. In this way our theological study cannot be said to have at any time emancipated itself from the Church's doctrine and magisterium.

itself is called "three-personality" and that in this context the
concept of "person" implies nothing more than what our starting
point has derived from the testimony of Scripture. This would
not yet take care of all difficulties, as the non-theological concept
of person possesses nowadays quite another meaning. But the
difficulties and the danger of tritheistic misunderstandings would
be reduced.

G. A New Relationship Between the Treatises "On the One God" and "On the Triune God"

Finally, our approach sheds a new light upon the problem of the
relation, the connection, and the distinction between the two
treaties, namely, *On the One God* and *On the Triune God*. It is
not as easy to distinguish these two treatises as was thought after
St. Thomas and under the influence of his example.[46] For when
we mean the expression "on the *one* God" literally, this treatise

46. For more details about the relation between the treatises *De Deo Uno*
and *De Deo Trino* in Thomas Aquinas, see F. Bourassa, *art. cit.* (note 14).
According to U. Horst (*Münchener Theologische Zeitschrift* 12 [1961],
note 56), Petrus of Poitiers had already used the same procedure in the
division and sequence of the treatises. In a later publication Horst asserts
even that Robert of Melun was the first to introduce a logical division of
the treatises; cp. *Die Trinität- und Gotteslehre des Robert van Melun*, Mainz,
1964, pp. 199f., 202 note 14. The last few years have also seen some
extensive investigation of the impact of salvation history on medieval
theology, especially for the doctrine of the Trinity. A great number of
excellent works have forced us to correct our conceptions in this respect.
Yet we have doubt about the trend of seeing numerous references to
salvation history in Thomas's doctrine of the Trinity—as in the writings of
Horst. For Horst never mentions the difficulties regarding the interpretation of *Summa Theologica* I, q. 43. Moreover, the discovery of so many
references to salvation history increases our surprise at the lack of emphasis
on these same aspects in Thomas's explicit doctrine of the Trinity. It
should be kept in mind, too, that the concept of salvation history—one so
important for theology today—should not be equated with the medieval
concept of "history of salvation." This would be to render a disservice to
the modern task of theology, especially regarding the doctrine of the
Trinity. For the real, factual problem in Thomas, see note 12 above.

does not speak only of God's essence and its unicity, but of the unity of the three divine persons, of the unity of the Father, the Son, and the Spirit, and not merely of the unicity of the divinity. We speak of the mediated unity, of which the Trinity is the proper consummation, and not of the unmediated unicity of the divine nature. For when we think of this nature as numerically one, we are not yet thinking *ipso facto* of the ground of God's tri-*unity*. However, since the treatise's title is *On the One God*, not *On the One Divinity*, we are from the start with the Father, the unoriginate origin of the Son and the Spirit. And this makes it properly impossible to put the two treatises without any connection one after the other, as is now frequently done.

Although we have thus established the methodically and practically correct starting point for a systematic doctrine of the Trinity, we have not yet discovered all the principles which must be considered in such a systematic doctrine. Hence a few more remarks are called for.

H. The Reality and the Doctrine of the Trinity as Mysteries

It is evident that the doctrine of the Trinity must always remain aware of its mysterious character, which belongs to the divine reality, insofar at least as we are concerned, now and forever, hence also in the blessed vision. For even in the vision God remains forever incomprehensible. This should be well understood. It does not mean only or mainly that this mystery consists in the special logical difficulty we experience in putting together the concepts used to express it. It means rather that this mystery is essentially identical with the mystery of the self-communication of God to us in Christ and in his Spirit.[47] Man understands him-

47. Cp. K. Rahner, "The Concept of Mystery in Catholic Theology," in *Theological Investigations*, volume IV, pp. 36–73.

self only when he has realized that he is the one to whom God communicates himself. Thus we may say that the mystery of the Trinity is the last mystery of our own reality, and that it is experienced precisely in this reality. This does not imply, of course, that we might, from this experience, by mere individual reflexion, conceptually objectivate the mystery. In line with this idea we might point out here[48] that the incomprehensible, primordial, and forever mysterious unity of transcendence through history and of history into transcendence holds its ultimate depths and most profound roots in the Trinity, in which the Father is the incomprehensible origin and the original unity, the "Word" his utterance into history, and the "Spirit" the opening up of history into the immediacy of its fatherly origin and end. And precisely this Trinity of salvation history, as it reveals itself to us by deeds, is the "immanent" Trinity.

This provides us with a methodical principle for the whole treatise on the Trinity. The Trinity is a mystery whose paradoxical character is preluded in the paradoxical character of man's existence. That is why it is meaningless to deny this mysteriousness, trying to hide it by an accumulation of subtle concepts and distinctions which only seem to shed more light upon the mystery, while in fact they feed man with verbalisms which operate as tranquilizers for *naïvely* shrewd minds, and dull the pain they feel when they have to worship the mystery without understanding it. Traditional discussions as to whether in God a person is constituted by the "relation" or by the "procession" are quarrels about subtleties which can in fact no longer be distinguished one from the other.

Hence if the critical reader gets the impression that the following explanation does not seem to come up to the conceptual subtlety of the classical theology of the Trinity (from Thomas up to, for example, Ruiz de Montoya), he is invited at least to

48. Cp. below, pp. 91ff.

consider the possibility that such a greater poverty and "lack of precision" has perhaps been adopted on purpose. On the other hand, our interpretation of the mysterious character of the Trinity and of its doctrinal expression entails that not every statement made about the Trinity should be submitted to the premature impatience of the rationalist and of the "kerygmatist" of mere verbalisms. When a true statement about the Trinity is correctly understood and translated into our life, the correctly understood theory points quite naturally towards real life, as lived in faith and in grace, in which the mystery of the triune God himself holds sway and which is not simply constituted by its conceptual objectivation.

What we have said above shows that the doctrine of the "missions" is from its very nature the starting point for the doctrine of the Trinity. No theology can in principle deny this, because it is a fact of salvation history that we know about the Trinity because the Father's Word has entered our history and has given us his Spirit. But this starting point should not only be tacitly *pre*supposed; the treatise should really start by positing it as such. Otherwise the meaning and the limits of *all* statements of this doctrine become unclear, and there is no way of avoiding the danger of wild and empty conceptual acrobatics. We shall start by showing that the economic Trinity *is* also already the immanent Trinity, and not merely presuppose this tacitly or add it as an afterthought. The question arises, then, whether a deeper understanding, which proceeds beyond this purely formal statement, can be reached through a "psychological" doctrine of the Trinity. This question will be examined in a later chapter.[49] At any rate, such "psychological" interpretation of the Trinity can be legitimate, important, and illuminating only if it shows how it derives from the real and only starting point of the whole doctrine of the Trinity and how it leads back to it.

49. Cp. below, pp. 115ff.

II. THE MAIN LINES
OF OFFICIAL TRINITARIAN DOCTRINE

Statements of the Church's magisterium have been elsewhere evaluated in their historical context,[1] but it may be worthwhile now to present them again in a *systematic* way. Such a systematization is not, of course, without its drawbacks and dangers. Taken out of their historical context these statements easily become unclear in their meaning and importance, even when one points out which are defined and which are not. Such texts are easily placed in a "system" which does not itself come from the magisterium, and are thus often seen in a false or doubtful light. In such a systematization of "Denzinger texts," the danger often arises that elements which are implicitly present in the living faith of the Church[2] (through Scripture, the liturgy, predication, other traditions, religious life) are overlooked or minimized, although they may be more important than many a Denzinger text which perhaps owes its origin to relatively secondary chance events of the history of dogma. We must pay attention to these and similar dangers in such a systematization.

Yet we need it. It is true that an authentically personal and at the same time theologically justified act of faith in the doctrine of the Trinity is not possible through a mere recital of the explicit doctrine of the magisterium, since every act of faith occurs unavoidably and necessarily under some "theology." Yet in order to make sure that this theology is the theology of the Church, we must from the start mold it after the doctrine of the magisterium. That is why we must first become acquainted with this doctrine.

1. Cp. *Mysterium Salutis*, volume II, pp. 146–220.
2. Cp. *ibid.*, pp. 132ff.

To this simple enumeration of texts we may already join a first attempt at reflexion, in which we try to find out what is being said in these official utterances, what remains unsaid or obscure, and so on. Such reflexion is not intended as critique, but as a first orientation, deriving from the official texts themselves, for the tasks which, according to these texts, remain urgent and become urgent for systematic theology.

A. The Trinity as Absolute Mystery

The dogma of the Trinity is an *absolute mystery* which we do not understand even after it has been revealed. The first part of this statement is an obvious conclusion from the doctrine of the First Vatican Council saying that there are "mysteries hidden in God which cannot be known unless revealed by God" (DS 3015f.), and that first and foremost among them comes the dogma of the Trinity (DS 3225; see also *Col. Lac.* VII, 507 c; 525 bc; DS 367, 616, 619 [the "ineffable Trinity"]). The second part of the statement contains the explanation given by the First Vatican Council about the nature of such mysteries (DS 3016), which are for this reason called "absolute." The Council insists against Rosmini that the mystery remains *forever* such (DS 3225). However, the concept of mystery is left undetermined, within the context of the Council's doctrine (and also elsewhere), except that it is opposed to the rational-conceptual intelligibility of a statement or to everyday empirical knowledge. Hence, when measured against the ideal of modern science, it looks like a negative value, not like the most basic positive character of that supreme kind of true knowledge which derives from man's openness to the lasting mystery.[3]

If the Trinity of the essentially and forever incomprehensible

3. Cp. K. Rahner, *Theological Investigations*, volume IV, pp. 36–73.

God is not merely an object within some neutral horizon of knowledge, if the *incomprehensible* God himself opens this horizon of knowledge while being himself essentially threefold, then "Trinity" and "mystery" belong essentially together, at least *after* we have heard about a Trinity from revelation, and supposing that we wish to develop a theology of knowledge. That Trinity is not just a case of this mystery. In a theology of knowledge the Trinity might deepen the very concept of mystery; in such a theology, God's very incomprehensibility might, as a *positive* predicate of our knowledge, be brought into inner proximity to the mystery of the Trinity.

B. The Meaning and Limits of the Employed Concepts

The basic concepts with which the mystery of the unity and Trinity of God are expressed in the ecclesiastical documents and in the utterances of the magisterium are: on the one hand, "person" ("subsistence": DS 501), on the other hand, "substance," "essence," "nature" (hence "divinity" and so on, also "supreme reality": DS 804), three concepts which are no longer distinguished in this context (cp. DS 73, 75, 112, 176, 188, 501, 525ff., 530f., 800, 803f., 1330, 1880, and so on).

I. THE HYPOTHESIS OF THE INTELLIGIBILITY
OF SUCH BASIC CONCEPTS AS A HERMENEUTIC PROBLEM

These two fundamental concepts of "person" and "essence" are not further explained in the ecclesiastical documents. Hence they are presupposed as intelligible in themselves. There are reasons for this presupposition, but they imply a problem. The presupposition that these words are intelligible may be based either on the fact that they have a general, stable sense, which it is easy to ascertain from everyday experience (such as in the words "bread" and "wine" in the doctrine of the Eucharist), or on the fact that the official doctrine of the Church presupposes that theology and the ordinary teaching of the Church have developed these concepts and accepted them with a certain meaning (as, for example, for the concept of "transubstantiation"), or finally on the fact that the meaning of the employed concepts is clear from their total context, at least in a first approximation. In the present case the first possibility is excluded; the second one is reducible to the third as to its origin; moreover, it does not (either in general or in the present case) allow us to arrive at a definition. Hence there remains only the third reason as an explanation of why the magisterium has not explained the use of these concepts.

That is also what history tells us.[4] The concepts are so established because we are first told that the Father is God; that the Son is God, and comes to meet us as such; and that the Holy Spirit is God and meets us as such; yet that in these three beings, who are God, only *one* God is given. To express *this* concept we are told that one and the same divinity (hence one "essence," one "substance," one "nature") is given to us in the three "persons." Thus two statements have been made which must now further be developed.

2. THE FUNCTION OF THE BASIC CONCEPTS AS A LOGICAL EXPLANATION OF REALITY

The words "person" and "essence" only tell us in another form the same thing that we already know from original experience and the statement of faith. We are told that we are dealing with God in his radical incomprehensible Godhead (Father), that this Godhead is really given to us in the Son and in the Holy Spirit;

4. Cp. *Mysterium Salutis*, volume II, pp. 166ff., 175ff.

yet that we are not to consider them as created intermediaries of this Godhead, nor merely as other words for the Godhead of the Father, who is with us through them. The historical origin of these concepts and the context in which they originated do not tell us whether they contain or may contain not only a logical, but also an ontic explanation.

By a *logical* explanation of a statement about a certain state of affairs, I mean an explanation which makes the statement in question clear, that is, more precise, less liable to be misunderstood. A logical explanation clarifies the statement independently of anything else. To put it roughly: the logical explanation explains by making more precise; it does not use one state of affairs to explain another one. Hence all the concepts used to explain that statement can be derived from it. This would still be the case if the *verbal* terminology used in the explanation were obtained elsewhere, provided only that it be well understood (explicitly or implicitly) that the employed terminology is meant only within the sense and scope of what is being explained.

An *ontic* explanation is one that takes into account *another* state of affairs, in such a way that this helps us to understand what is to be explained. It helps to avoid misunderstandings by listing the cause of something, the exact and concrete way in which something comes about. Thus when everything turns dark before my eyes, I can ontically explain this fact by attributing it to a turning-off of the light, or to the physiological atrophy of my optic nerve.

It follows at once that a logical explanation can be understood only if it refers always to the statement which is to be explained. The ontic explanation, on the other hand (as is clear from our simple example), is not based on anything that needs explaining; it stands of itself, since it takes another state of affairs into account. Yet, though the logical explanation refers continually back to the statement in need of explanation, and although it lives from this reference and turns into empty verbalism and conceptual rationalism without it, it is and remains a very important kind of explanation. We cannot show here why this is the case. Everyone knows this at heart and makes use of such explanations.

He who does biblical theology wishes to say exactly what the Scripture says, yet he cannot simply repeat the words of Scripture. In this respect, it seems to me, the only but essential difference between Protestant and Catholic theology is this: that for the Catholic theologian the logical explanation of the words of Scripture by the Church can definitely become a statement of faith; whereas for the Protestant theologian it remains basically theology, and it may always be revised and reversed. Let us add this, however: that although a logical explanation can become for us an unchangeable dogma, we see that even then it differs qualitatively from Scripture. Furthermore, not only insofar as it validly binds our faith, but also for its meaning and interpretation, such a formula always looks back to the words of Scripture (or of the original tradition). It is also true that this word of Scripture remains alive and normative only if, through a dogmatically binding (logical) explanation, it abides in the ever-changing historical situation.

The question is now whether the two concepts of substance and essence provide us only with a logical explanation, or also with an ontic one. The explicit answer to this question may wait until we systematically explain the doctrine of the Trinity. But it is very important to see the question itself. At any rate, we may say this: insofar as these concepts belong to the *dogma* of the Church,[5] they intend to be only a logical, not an ontic explanation. They are an explanation of the state of affairs which they wish to express—one which, in Scripture and in the pre-Nicean tradition, and even in later doctrinal pronouncements of the

5. For this concept and for the following considerations, cp. *Mysterium Salutis*, volume I, esp. pp. 686–703.

Church, could be expressed and has in fact been expressed (and as it still may be expressed today), without reference to such concepts. This does not mean that they are not important even for the expression of the dogma as such. They are quite well suited, almost necessary, to safeguard the dogma against tritheistic or modalistic or subordinationalistic misunderstanding. This safeguard function itself shows that these two concepts, rather than directly representing for us the thing which is meant, refer us to the dark mystery of God.

We may also draw another conclusion. When we wonder what these concepts really mean, we must say that, as concepts of dogma as such, in their "logical" explanation, they always refer back to the origin from which they come: the experience of faith which assures us that the incomprehensible God is really, as he is in himself, given to us in the (for us) twofold reality of Christ and his Spirit, and which forbids us to think of this (for us) double reality (the way in which God's self-communication comes to us) in a modalistic way, as merely the result of a mental distinction deriving from our intelligence. For this would do away with the self-communication of God; it would no longer let God come to us as he is in himself (thus modalism and Arianism belong together). Hence insofar as the *dogmatically* necessary content of both concepts is concerned, nothing should be introduced into them except that which follows ultimately from our basic axiom, that which comes *from the fact* that the "economic" Trinity is *for us* first known and first revealed, that it is the "immanent" Trinity and that of it we can know with dogmatic certitude only what has been revealed about the former. We shall later inquire whether it is possible to invest even more speculative content into these concepts, so that the "logical" may become an "ontic" explanation, a theological explanation, one not proposed by the magisterium.

3. CAN THE CONCEPT OF "PERSON" BE REPLACED?

In principle, the concepts of essence and substance are not simply irreplaceable for the formulation of the trinitarian dogma. This is, of course, true for the past; yet not only for the past, but also *in principle*, absolutely, for the future fate of the dogmatic formulation. Since they are but the "logical" explanation of the more primitive revelation, it is *a priori* not impossible that *this* kind of explanation may be presented also by means of other concepts. Of course, these other possible concepts cannot be invented arbitrarily and *so* replace the present ones. They should refer to the *same* lasting reality, reproduce the content of the earlier "simpler" formulation, and defend it against misunderstandings. Concretely it is hardly conceivable that the concepts of "essence" and "substance," in their most formal meaning, should eventually be replaced by better concepts. Yet it is possible that, in another conceptual framework, whether pre-scientific or derived from philosophical reflexion, a few aspects may come out more clearly than hitherto. Such concepts would then be better suited for the trinitarian dogma. Of this kind would be concepts that are less static, more onto-*logical*, referring more to a spiritual rather than to a thinglike reality.

In this context the problem is more serious for the concept of "person" (and "hypostasis").[6] Its history up to the time it was used in the trinitarian dogma shows that its meaning and also its usefulness for this dogma are not quite clearcut. The concept of "person" has continued to have a further history *after* its introduction into dogmatic thought and the dogma of the Church. Thus the word has acquired shades of meaning to which our concept may *not* be tied within this dogmatic formula. Thus, as we said above, when nowadays we hear of "three persons,"

6. Cp. below, pp. 8off., esp. p. 103.

we connect, almost necessarily, with this expression the idea of three centers of consciousness and activity, which leads to a heretical misunderstanding of the dogma. It is true, of course, that theology may theoretically keep such modifications of meaning away from *its* concept of person, by clearly formulated "definitions." But in fact the Church is not the mistress and guide of such a history of concepts. Thus in principle it is not apriorily impossible that the word may develop historically in such a way that, at long last, despite the theoretical right of the magisterium to "regulate the language of the community," a right which is included in every dogmatic decision, it may be impossible to use the word in the kerygma without incurring the danger of tritheistic misunderstanding. Even at a time when the Church's magisterium rightly upholds this concept (the word) by authoritatively determining the terminology in behalf of a *common* confession of the truth, the theologian is not forbidden, but should rather consider it a duty, to examine whether the word "person" is really always concretely irreplaceable. He has to explain the word. He must say what is and what it not meant *here* by the word, he must distinguish it from its changing profane meaning, and thus, on account of these changes in meaning, his situation and task is forever a new one. Perhaps he may even summarize these distinctions and explanations themselves in some new word, no longer the word "person." In its correct, better adapted meaning, such a word may be more precisely and easily understood, hence kerygmatically more useful than the word "person." The systematic presentation of the doctrine of the Trinity must at least give some thought to this kind of problem.

C. A Systematic Summary
of Official Trinitarian Doctrine

After these two preparatory remarks we must now say *what* is stated in the official doctrine of the Church. This brings up the problem of the structure of this exposition, which is not simply a question of didactic simplicity and clarity. A *double starting point* is possible: we may, with scriptural theology, the older creeds, and Eastern theology, start with the one God who is, and insofar as he is the Father.

Or we may, as with later official explanations by the Church, start from the Trinity, that is, from the *one* God whose *one* essence subsists in three persons. We prefer the former starting point for reasons which should be stated now and developed later more systematically. Using the concepts of "essence" and "person," we shall therefore now set forth the official doctrine of the Church.

I. STATEMENTS ABOUT GOD AS THE FATHER

(a) *The Confession of the Father*. The Church confesses one almighty God who appears to her as the active Lord of salvation history and as creator of all finite reality (DS 125, 150), and confesses him as the "Father" (DS 1–5 and not 6!; also 10–17, 19, 21ff., 25, 27–30, 36, 40ff., 44, 46, 48, 50f., 55, 60f., 64, 71, 125, 139, 150, 470, 1862). "I believe in the one God, the Father almighty." We may, of course, also start with the confession of the Trinity. However, this should not mean that somehow there lies "behind" the three persons a "godhead" which is properly intended by the confession and subsequently gives rise to the threefold personality (cp. DS 803, 973f.). The confession and the

58

religious act intend the concreteness of the salvific reality. But the Trinity, as *such* a "three-ness" and thus conceived as unity, is a later notion, since it puts the "three" together into a unity with respect precisely to that (namely, "person") through which they are properly distinct. All this explains why it is quite legitimate, even in a systematization of the doctrine of the Church, to begin as in the ancient creeds with the confession of the Father.

(*b*) *God Known as Father.* However, the question arises at once: Is this "Father" accessible to confession and faith in such a way that he may be confessed as first by kerygma, faith, and creed? Of course, he is mentioned in the first place in the creeds because of the development of the history of salvation and revelation. The God of the old covenant—ὁ Θεός, as such—is already known and confessed in the experience of salvation and revelation. About *this* God, who is already known, who has already assumed a relation to man, we find out, through the event of the New Testament, that he sends us his Son and the Spirit of his Son.[7] We must avoid the misunderstanding that the one who acts in the Old Testament, insofar as he is the concrete partner, is the triune God. "Triune God" and "Trinity" are legitimate but secondary concepts which, after the events, synthesize the concrete experience of salvation and revelation in a "short formula." The experience of God in revelation, together with the transcendental moment of the dynamism of the created spirit towards God, intends originally and necessarily the *concrete* God, and him as necessarily, simply, and absolutely *unoriginate*.[8] If one does not

7. This is undeniable for the theology of the Old and of the New Testament. Cp. K. Rahner, "*Theos* in the New Testament," in *Theological Investigations*, volume I, pp. 79–148, 92ff., 125ff.

8. Of course, before the revelation of the Trinity, the total unoriginatedness cannot yet be differentiated into aseity and innascibility (the fact of being *absolutely* ἀγέννητος and ἄναρχος), but the second moment of the Father's originlessness is necessarily affirmed in a formally implicit way as soon as it is known that there *must* be a "principle without principle."

arbitrarily set up an "absolute subsistence"[9] which smacks of "quaternity" (DS 804), then this concrete unoriginate one (whether or not one knows that he is the origin of the two divine processions) is precisely he who, as soon as this knowledge is available, is the Father. Of course, the Father, as the concrete God of the Old Testament, is known as Father only when the Son is known. Then we understand also that he acts and can act[10] only in the unity with the Son and the Holy Spirit ("who spoke through the prophets"). But this changes nothing of the fact that, when and insofar as the Trinity has not yet been revealed, the concrete God, who is necessarily conceived as unoriginate, and with whom the history of pre-trinitarian revelation is concerned, is the "Father."

(c) *The Father of the Son.* Through the encounter in faith with Jesus Christ, the "Son" as such, and with the Holy Spirit, as

---

This is the case in every true knowledge of God. For the explicit assertion of the Father's unoriginatedness, cp. DS 60, 75, 441, 485, 490, 525, 527, 569, 572, 683, 800, 1330f.: ἀγέννητος, *non genitus, a nullo originem ducit (sumpsit), principium sine principio.*

9. For an historical, factual, and critical discussion of this topic, cp. H. Mühlen, *Person und Appropriation,* pp. 39f., with note 13, pp. 47f. and *passim.* Also C. Sträter, "Le point de départ du traité thomiste de la Trinité," in *Sciences Ecclésiastiques* 14 (1962), pp. 71–87, esp. p. 76, note 15.

10. This is true first because of the unity of the divine essence, on account of which an outward activity (a real efficient activity) is always the one action of the Father, Son, and Holy Spirit, of the triune God. Moreover, the self-revelation of the Father as *such,* which (for reasons that cannot be explained here) cannot be simply the communication of some conceptual knowledge, but must be a real salvific activity for man, can (*pace* Augustine and the subsequent theology) always only be a self-communication of the Father through the Son in the Holy Spirit (cp. DS 140: the 14th and 15th anathema of the first Sirmian formula of 357; further DS 1621, 2229: "Invisibiliis," which only later becomes an assertion about the Trinity: thus DS 683). For even the *real* self-communication of the Father as such, which is presupposed by the conceptual-verbal one, is, by the very nature of the Trinity, necessarily the communication of the Son in the Spirit if "Fatherhood" means a mere "relation" to the Son and the Spirit.

the innermost principle of our sonship and of our absolute proximity to God,[11] this unoriginate God is experienced as the *Father of the Son*, as "generating principle," as source, origin, and principle of the whole godhead (DS 490, 525, 3326). This will be still further developed in the following considerations.

2. STATEMENTS ABOUT THE SON

(*a*) *Basic Declarations of the Church Doctrine*. This "Father," then, has an (only) Son.[12] The Son is "begotten" by him, that is, not made "out of nothing." He *is* through the communication, deriving from the Father's essence (hence not through a decision, or through outside necessity; DS 71, 526), of the Father's own divine and total essence, of his "substance," of his "nature." Thus he is "consubstantial" with the Father, since the Father communicates everything to him (except his "Fatherhood"; DS 1301, 1986). Thus he shares the Father's eternity. Although ecclesiastical usage shows no *preference* (DS 2698) for the concept of "Logos," according to the Scriptures this relation of the "Son" to the "Father" should be understood as that of the "Logos" ("Word," "Wisdom") to him who through this Logos expresses himself in salvation history, hence also "immanently" (DS 40, 55, 113, 144, 147, 178, 250ff., 427, 502f., 852, 3326).

(*b*) *Differentiations in Jesus' Self-Interpretation as the Son*. From biblical theology, or more precisely from the self-understanding

11. For this starting point of the knowledge of God as the Father we must here refer to Christology and the doctrine of grace. We speak frequently and on purpose of "experiencing," because, although the conceptual expression is implied as a constitutive and indispensable moment in the self-revelation of God as the Father, this expression itself is a moment of a real event, the experience of Jesus Christ and of his Spirit.

12. In order to avoid too many references to DS we invite the reader to consult that work's systematic index. We shall make only those references which do not seem to be too obvious.

of the historical Jesus,[13] one can also gain an *original* real understanding of such statements as the above. Jesus knew that his relation to God, whom he called his "Father," distinguished his sonship from that of other men.[14] Nonetheless it remains methodically dangerous, even if ultimately correct, to understand at once and from the very start this unique sonship, which the Synoptics show us to have been known by Jesus, as referring only, in Jesus' own understanding of himself, to the eternal generation of the Logos. Jesus knew himself first as the concrete One, who stands before the Father and meets us as the Son (as such). Hence it would be dangerous to separate, at the very beginning, various aspects of this concrete reality (his human, created "nature") from the whole which he *himself* calls "Son." *His* concept may be much more complex. The Sonship of which we speak in the Church's doctrine may be an ontological ground and background of what *he* means by "Son," but it does not necessarily have to be the whole of what *he* means by "Son." May we really say without more ado that from the concept of Son of the synoptic Jesus we must eliminate his obedience to the Father, his adoration, his submission to the Father's unfathomable will?[15] For we eliminate them when we explain this kind of behavior in him only through the hypostatic union as such. They are then

13. Cp. the article of F. J. Schierse in *Mysterium Salutis*, volume II, pp. 89ff.

14. There is no need here to present biblical Christology in detail, especially since a distinction must be made between the self-understanding of the "synoptic" Jesus and its theological interpretation in Jesus' discourses in John and in apostolic Christology (primitive community, Paul, John). We must simply refer to the biblical starting point of the official Church documents about the consubstantiality of Christ. If we wish to understand these documents correctly, this starting point must always again be clarified.

15. For the exegetical problems, cp. F. J. Schierse, *loc. cit.*; B. M. F. Van Iersel, *Der "Sohn" in den synoptischen Jesusworten*, Leiden 1964; R. Schnackenburg in *Lexikon für Theologie und Kirche* IX (1964), pp. 852ff. (Lit.); F. Hahn, *Christologische Hoheitstitel*, Göttingen, ²1964, pp. 319ff. (Lit.), esp. pp. 332f.

properties of the Son, but not constitutive moments of his son-ship. We mean, of course, of the sonship as Jesus meant it, not of its ontological presupposition, which nowadays we call the "metaphysical" sonship.

(c) *The Son as the "Absolute Bringer of Salvation" and as Self-Communication of the Father.* We may *first* state without hesitation that Jesus knew himself as the concrete man, as "the Son" as such—but, in a unique way, in the sense that through him, as the "absolute bringer of salvation"[16] (the Messiah in a radical sense, which differs basically from that of a prophet), the Father, his will, his salvation, his pardon, his kingdom "are there" in absolute and final proximity, that they are communicated to us. The Son is first (as a concept which is concretely identical with the "Messiah" when the latter is understood not as "prophet," but as "absolute bringer of salvation") the self-communication of the Father to the world in such a way that in this Son he is radically *there* and that his self-communication entails, as an effect produced by itself, its radical acceptance. The *Son* is the economic (historical) self-communication of the Father.[17]

16. On the question why the concept of the absolute bearer of salvation necessarily implies the hypostatic union, see K. Rahner, *Theological Investigations*, volume IV, pp. 67ff. Also A. Darlap, *Mysterium Salutis*, volume I, pp. 59ff., 99ff.

17. The relation of this self-communication to the one given in the Spirit must be considered later. When we say that the Son *is* the salvific *self*-communication of the Father, we do not say that the Father has appeared and has united himself "hypostatically" to some human nature. Such an idea would make sense only in the hypothesis that the Father too might incarnate himself. But this is an arbitrary hypothesis which, in final analysis, does away with the mystery of the Trinity, with the identity of the immanent and economic Trinity, and with the possibility of understanding the former from the latter. If we may say, speaking "immanently," that the Son is the self-expression of the Father, the word of the Father (not of the Godhead), we should also be able to say it "economically," and only in this assertion would we understand what the "immanent" relation is between Father and Son.

(d) *"Economic" and "Immanent" Self-Communication to the Son.* If we use the Greek-scholastic terminology, we may say: the "procession" of the Son as self-communication of the divine reality of the Father is two things at once. It is first of all, for us, the economic, free self-communication of the divine reality to Jesus as the "absolute bringer of salvation." It is also the necessary "immanent" self-communication of the divine reality, the Father expressing himself in such a way that this utterance exists from all eternity and of necessity, as the Word of such a possible free self-expression to the world. The "immanent" self-communication becomes perceptible, and its meaning, although remaining mysterious, becomes intelligible, in the "economic" self-communication.

In order that these statements may be more fully understood, two points should be noted: (1) the "Father" (God as such) is there, he communicates himself as he is; yet he is the unoriginate, who keeps to himself, who remains the incomprehensible; the "Father," by expressing himself and thus in this self-expression (first economically) distinguishing himself from his self-communication; (2) this distinction "pre-exists" to the free gratuitous self-communication of God (of the absolutely unoriginate, of the Father) as its possibility. The Λόγος ἐνδιάθετος is the condition of the possibility of the Λόγος προφορικός. This does not make of the Logos a mere principle of creation. For if the *verbum prolativum* (cp. DS 144, 147) is uttered *freely, thus* having its condition in the Father's immanent Word, it must have an "immanent" sense and a meaning for the Father himself. Otherwise the Father's self-expression *ad extra* would either no longer be a free grace, or no "immanent" word could pre-exist in relation to it as the condition of its possibility. Here lies the critical point of the whole question. Why is the Son as the word of the free self-expression of the Father to the world necessarily also the Λόγος ἐνδιάθετος of the Father? Why does the possibility of the Father's self-expression to the world, even as a mere possibility, already imply an inner "differentiation" in God himself?

First we may simply point out that the experience of the absolute proximity of the God who communicates himself in Christ is already interpreted in this way by the theology of the New Testament. This theology knows already of a descent Christology [*Deszendenzchristologie*] as an interpretation of an ascent Christology [*Aszendenzchristologie*] in the Synoptics and in the discourses of the Acts of the Apostles. But *how* and *why* did such an interpretation arise—a "theology" developed within the very framework of the history of revelation? Taking a leaf from this biblical interpretation itself we may say: Jesus knew of himself in a peculiar way as the "Son" *as well* with respect to the Father *as also* with respect to men. But this would be impossible if he were simply the Father making himself present and giving himself in a human reality. Let us suppose that, speaking in the traditional terminology, we should, in some kind of Sabellian way, allow the human reality to subsist hypostatically in the Father. In that case we could still in this humanity conceive of a spiritual, free, created subjectivity which might also refer to the Father in adoration, obedience, and so on, exactly as scholastic theology conceives of this humanity in its relation to the Logos. It might call this origin in which it subsists "Father." But as the concrete presence of the Father it could not with respect to *man* experience and express itself as the *Son* of the Father.

These brief and stammering words are not yet intended as a precise doctrine of the sonship of the Son and his relation to the absolutely unoriginate God. Our sole intention was to underline briefly some problems in the ecclesiastical statements and to point to the *really first* starting point, derived from the history of revelation, for a genuine understanding of the expression *"immanent" Son of the Father.* Here too it is clear that the understanding of the "immanent" Trinity must come from the "economic" Trinity.[18]

3. STATEMENTS ABOUT GOD AS THE "SPIRIT"

(a) *Basic Statements of the Magisterium.* The gift of the Father through the Son (DS 570, 1522, 1529f., 1561, 1690, 3330), in which he communicates himself *to us* in immediate proximity and through which he causes us to accept this self-communication, is the "Spirit" of the Father and the Son.[19] As self-communication of God he is God as given in love and powerful in us in love. Hence he possesses the one and same essence as the Father, he is God, yet distinct from Father and Son. He proceeds from the Father and the Son through an eternal communication of the divine essence as the act of the Father and the Son. If we wish to mention also the relation of the unoriginate Father to the uttered, begotten Son and the unity of the act of communication, we might also and more precisely phrase it as follows (DS 1300f., 1986): the Spirit proceeds from the Father through the Son. This

---

18. The biblical Christology required for this cannot be once more explained here. But we must insist that the transition from the self-expression of the historic Jesus to the doctrine of the "pre-existence" of the Son, in Paul and John, must be made intelligible. This is a problem not only for apologetics or fundamental theology, but also for dogmatic theology. For although, dogmatically speaking, the pre-existence Christology of Paul and John is to be considered as divine revelation, it is not a strictly original datum of revelation (cp. Rahner, *Schriften*, volume V, pp. 33–53, esp. pp. 33f.) but inspired theology, developed from Jesus' self-interpretation in connection with the experience of his resurrection. When we inquire about the *reason* and the *justification* of this "theological development," we also inquire (and we discover a guiding principle to answer the question) *what* is properly meant by this pre-existence, that is, by the eternal relation of Father to Son within God.

19. Here too we must for further details refer to the theology of grace, to ecclesiology, and to the doctrine of the sacraments. For the texts in DS we refer once more in general to the systematic index B 2bc, except for cases where an explicit reference to particular texts seemed indicated.

communication should not be called "begetting" (DS 485, 490, 527, 617), for this might lead to the misunderstanding that there are two "Sons," or to the merely modalistic view that the "Spirit" is only the relation of the elevated Son to men, the manner in which he communicates himself to us. Neither should the Spirit, as the gift of the Father and the Son, be modalistically conceived as the way in which the Father himself appears. Therefore the Spirit is not "unoriginate" (*ingenitus*; cp. DS 71, 75, 683). The original character of the divine self-communication which constitutes the Spirit is stated only negatively in the official Church doctrine. We are only told that it is not a "begetting." Thus it is characterized by the general concept of "procession" which may also be attributed to the Son. Positively this "procession" is mentioned only with caution, it is conceived as the procession of the mutual love of Father and Son, and in this sense it originates "voluntarily" (DS 573, 3326, 3331).

(*b*) *The "Procession" of the Holy Spirit.* In order to understand the various texts about the distinction of the Spirit from Father and Son and about his "procession," we must *mutatis mutandis* repeat what we said about the Son.[20] The starting point is the experience of faith, which makes us aware that, through what we call "Holy Spirit," God (hence the Father) *really* communicates *himself* as love and forgiveness, that he produces this self-communication in us and maintains it by himself. Hence the "Spirit" must be God himself.[21] This reality of salvation history is not only modally, that is, subsequently, on account of its recipient,

20. For more details about the exegetical background, cp. F. J. Schierse, "Die Neutestamentliche Trinitätsoffenbarung," in *Mysterium Salutis*, volume II, pp. 97ff., esp. pp. 113–125.

21. The doctrine of grace must show in more detail that the doctrine of "created" (infused and "habitual") grace, as it prevails in Latin theology since the reaction against Peter Lombard, does not contradict this biblical and patristic basic conception, or should, at least, not reject it. Cp. Willig, *loc. cit.*, pp. 259f.; M. Flick and Z. Alszeghy, *loc. cit.*, pp. 561–606 (Lit.).

but of itself, and despite its real divine character, distinct from the Father who gives and from the Son who mediates. We demonstrate. this, according to our fundamental trinitarian axiom, through the fact[22] that the concrete Christ distinguishes this gift from himself not only with respect to God (the Father) but also with respect to those who receive the Spirit.

4. THE RELATIONS WITHIN THE TRINITY

If Father, Son, and Spirit possess for us *and* in themselves the one same godhead, and if on the other hand they are not simply the same someone (or something), then their relation should, without losing its mysterious character, be interpreted conceptually in such a way that we may say all that follows.

(*a*) *The Concept of "Relation."* Father, Son, and Spirit are only "relatively" distinct;[23] that is, in their distinction they should not be conceived as constituted by something which would mean a distinction previous to their mutual relations and serving as their foundation.[24] For such a distinction, previous to the relations as

22. We are not speaking here of the *whole* of scriptural theology. In its triadic formulas it undoubtedly distinguishes the Spirit from the Father and the Son, as well as the Son from the Father. It follows that if it recognizes an economic duality, and a duality which is *immanent* in the latter, it also teaches an immanent Trinity. The only question is to what extent this whole biblical theology was already implicitly contained in germ in Jesus' understanding of himself and was thus legitimately derived from it in Scripture. For biblical theology, cp. F. J. Schierse, *loc. cit.*, pp. 118ff. Also on this whole problem see H. Mühlen, *Der Heilige Geist als Person*, Münster, 1963.

23. Cp. DS 528, 532, 570.

24. In the case of "Father-Son" (Word) the mutual relation of the concepts is evident. This is not so true of the Spirit. The remark is explicitly made in DS 570 (XVIth Council of Toledo, 693), and there is an attempt to overcome the difficulty by using the concept of "gift." This concept was clearly understood in the economic sense, yet this was not regarded as a difficulty against the characterization of the Spirit as distinct from Father and Son.

such, would add something to the one divinity and thus do away with its absolute infinity and unity. This shows that the concept of "relation" is, at least at first, a *logical*, not an ontological explanation (cp. section B. above), hence that this concept does not contribute to the basic statement about the Trinity something which is intelligible in itself, so as to make the statement more understandable by means of an ontologically previous concept. Its purpose is to protect the same truth (the one and same God is given in the Father, the Son, and the Spirit, yet these three words do not mean one and the same thing) against tritheistic or modalistic misinterpretations, by means of a formulation, which derives from within the other, previous one. Hence really to understand the concept of "relation" as used *here* (at least at first), we must not consult any general ontology, but return to the more primitive statement which we have to defend against such misunderstandings. Whether it is possible to pass from such a logical explanation to an ontological one, so as to refute the famous rationalistic objections against the Trinity, may thus be a matter for discussion. Against these objections too the most convincing method is to return to the more primitive statement about our experience of the "economic" Trinity.

Of course, by pointing to the relationality of the divine persons we derive some help against the basic logical difficulty against the doctrine of the Trinity, namely, how there can be three really distinct persons in God, if each one of them is really identical with the one, simple essence of God. Appealing to the pure relationality of the persons does not intend positively to solve this difficulty. Otherwise we might as well solve the mystery of the Trinity rationalistically. This appeal wishes only to *show negatively and defensively* that the basic difficulty—how two things which are identical with a third are not identical with each other—cannot, in the present case, be shown to be insuperable. Of course, generally speaking, it would be desirable that theology should not at this late point, in this context, begin to treat the logical problem of the impossibility of distinguishing certain statements.[25] Such an examination should be carried out in a more general and thorough discussion of the problem.

More precisely, a negative defense of the basic logical difficulty regarding the doctrine of the Trinity proceeds as follows: that while it is obvious that two *absolute* realities cannot be identical with a third without being really identical with each other, this disparity cannot be shown with evidence when we are dealing with two "mere" and opposed relations, which are really identical with an absolute reality (God's essence). Of course, it is not enough to point out that in God the relations are "virtually" distinct from the essence and that this suffices to make them not identical *with each other*, although they are really identical with the essence. For either this "virtual" (modal, formal, *etcetera*) distinction is a *mental* one, in which case the fundamental difficulty persists at first; or it is a *real* distinction, however one may understand it, in that it posits in the thing itself a duality of distinct realities, in which case the trinitarian basic axiom of the Council of Florence (DS 1331) has to be given up and an heretical "quaternity" in God can no longer be avoided. The virtual distinction of "essence" and "person" in God may contribute to solving the basic difficulty only if we also emphasize at once the fact that, in the case of this virtual distinction, we do not have a distinction between two absolute realities, but a virtual distinction between an absolute and a relative reality. More about this presently.

Nevertheless, pointing to the relationality contributes something to the basic problem. First, we may say this: if every relation

25. Cp. V. Richter, "Logik und Geheimnis," in *Gott in Welt*, volume I, Freiburg, 1964, pp. 188–206. The theological problem is taken up directly by B. Lonergan, *De Deo Trino*, volume II, Rome, 1964, pp. 139–143.

is really identical with God's absolute essence, the persons are distinct only through their *esse ad* (their being relative to) and the three opposed relative *esse ad* are of the same perfection. Hence should anyone object that one person does not have the same perfection as the others, since he does not possess the formal determinations of the two others, this objection cannot be well taken, whether or not one considers such an *esse ad* formally as such to be a "perfection." Catholic theologians do not agree on this point, but all agree that in God the relation is real only through its identity with the real divine essence. For these reasons, each person is as perfect as the others.

As for the difficulty deriving from the principle of "compared identity," the following points may be made.

(1) In the case of the Trinity we are first concerned with a formal identity of nature and person. The dogma is not in conflict with the axiom in question, insofar as this axiom says that two realities which are *formalissime* identical with a third are identical with each other. This axiom expresses simply the principle of contradiction, which is self-evident, insofar as we are concerned with realities of formally the same content.

(2) We must grant the fact that when two absolute realities (*esse in*) are identical with a third, they are also identical with one another. For in the case of absolute realities there is no reason why they should differ when their whole reality and intelligibility is, as absolute (as not-relative), identical with a third.

(3) The case is different, however, when two opposed relations are given. In this event they must be really distinct from one another. Yet they possess also a content (an intelligibility) which does not let them *simply and altogether* (*re et ratione*) coincide with the absolute reality with which they are supposed really (*re*) to be identical. In this event the relations are not distinct by what they posit "absolutely" each for itself, but through their opposition as such. That which is absolute possesses, as it were,

its content in itself, whereas that which is relative is constituted by its relatedness to another, and in the case of real relative opposition by its necessary distinction from the opposed relation to which it refers. Hence despite its real identity with an absolute, an identity which is presupposed, a relative reality possesses a content through which it is distinct from other, opposed relations. Hence in our case we presuppose that two opposed relations can be really identical with something absolute. Such a presupposition cannot be positively verified in the empirical domain of finite reality, nor can it be shown to be positively contradictory, unless one already admits that the basic difficulty is insuperable.

Now if we accept the above presupposition, then the "principle of compared identity" cannot provide a *peremptory* argument *against* the doctrine of the Trinity. For this principle derives its meaning and its strength from the principle of the *formal* identity or from the principle of contradiction. Only if an absolute reality would posit two other absolute contents, which are really identical with it, will these two contents ultimately be formally identical with each other. It would not be possible for them to be really distinct from each other, without clashing with the formal principle of contradiction. On the other hand, when an absolute is really identical with two opposed relatives, this real identity does not yet imply a formal identity of the two opposed relatives. Their real identity cannot be apodictically demonstrated from the formal principle of contradiction.

(*b*) *The Identity of the Essence and Distinction of the Three.* It follows that we must say that the Father, Son, and Spirit are identical with the one godhead and are "relatively" distinct from one another. These three as distinct are constituted only by their relatedness to one another, so that the axiom which asserts the identity of the essence *and* the distinction of the three may also be formulated (as Anselm was the first to do and as done by the Council of Florence) as follows: in God everything is one except where there is relative opposition (DS 1330).[26] Hence these opposed relativities are also concretely identical with both "communications" ("processions") as seen from both sides, through which the Father communicates the divine essence to the Son and through the Son to the Spirit, or through which the latter two receive this communicated essence. The doctrine of the Church does not consider the question whether it can be more basically said of the three that they are constituted by the "processions" or by the "relations."

5. THE BASIC MEANING OF THE CONCEPTS "HYPOSTASIS" AND "PERSON" IN THE OFFICIAL DOCTRINE OF THE CHURCH

Insofar (and only insofar!) as one can see these three in their diversity and nonetheless bring them as such under one concept, the doctrine of the Church speaks of three "subsistences" ("hypostases"; cp. DS 112, 501).

(a) *Hypostasis*. We said that the doctrine of the Church speaks of *three* "hypostases," or "subsistences." It makes no attempt to explain independently from this context what a "hypostasis" or "subsistence" is. Hence to understand this concept theologically in this context we are referred to the concrete three, with whom we are concerned in our experience of salvation and also to our understanding of the one identical godhead (divine "essence") which we attribute to the three. If we draw our inspiration from

26. "In Deo omnia sunt unum, ubi non obviat relationis oppositio" (In God everything is one where there is no relative opposition). For a correct understanding of this assertion cp. H. Mühlen, *Person und Appropriation*, pp. 43ff; for the pre-history of the axiom: M. Schmaus, *Katholische Dogmatik*, volume I, Munich ⁶1960, pp. 494f.; B. Lonergan, *De Deo Trino*, volume II, pp. 201–204.

this starting point, hence also from the basic axiom of our theology of the Trinity, and if we are not simply content to use the two above words without further inquiry, then one way of expressing what we mean might be to say that these statements regarding the one same God, speak first ("economically") of three concrete ways of being given, of givenness, and then ("immanently") of three relative concrete ways of existing of the one and same God.[27] The second expression can be understood only by referring it to the first, for it adds explicitly to the former that the "immanent" actual possibility of this threefold way of being given is, despite God's free gratuitous trinitarian self-communication, forever given in God, belonging therefore necessarily and "essentially" to him. Should one say that, according to the economic basic starting point, "Son" and "Spirit" should be understood as manners of givenness of the Father, this must not be taken as contradicting what is meant by "subsistence" and "hypostasis." For, on the one hand, it cannot be denied "economically" that the Father himself gives himself in the Son and the Spirit, that he is thus "immanently" himself insofar as he has Son and Spirit as the recipients of *his* essence; on the other hand, insofar as he is unoriginate, we have already said that the Father himself has a manner of being given and of existing which distinguishes him from Son and Spirit, but which yet does not properly precede his relation to either of them.

27. Or "ways of being," as Barth prefers. We may already remark here that, when we speak of the concrete reality of the Father, the Son, and the Spirit, we also mean the divine (absolute) essence. That is why we cannot simply speak of "ways of being." What is meant here *most formally* is that which the hypostasis wishes to express, *as distinguished from God's essence*. We might call it the "substantiality," if "subsistence" were not already a relatively abstract term. The same remark applies to "hypostasis," which means originally not that which subsists, but the fact of subsisting. Hence there is no reason why we should not call the fact of subsisting a "way of existing (or of being)." The Cappadocians too had already spoken of τρόποι τῆς ὑπάρξεως.

(*b*) *"Person."* These three "hypostases" ("subsistences") are also called "persons" (DS 73, 75, 173, 176, 525ff., 530f., 800, 803f., 1330, 1880). We shall not consider here the problem of the history of this concept, nor in what way it entered into statements about the Trinity, nor the subtle changes in its meaning throughout this history, with their danger of modalistic overtones. Let us first make it clear that in the official doctrine of the Church this term says nothing which has not yet been said with the word "hypostasis." This is already evident from the fact that both words are used as synonyms. Furthermore, it is evident that the element of consciousness, which nowadays and from long ago is almost spontaneously connected with the concept,[28] does not belong to it in our context, insofar as it expresses the formal moment of this concept as distinguished from the *essence* of God. Otherwise the "three" would also have to be said of this "element of consciousness." But there exists in God only *one* power, *one* will, only one self-presence, a unique activity, a unique beatitude, and so forth.[29] Hence self-awareness is not a moment which distinguishes the divine "persons" one from the other, even though each divine "person," as concrete, possesses a self-consciousness. Whatever would mean three

28. This is also often tacitly, but wrongly, presupposed in some "demonstrations" by which biblical theology tries to establish the "personality" of the (immanent) Son and Spirit, when they wish to demonstrate a "personality" of the Son and the Spirit which is distinct from that of the Father.

29. Cp. DS 3, 71, 73, 144f., 172, 177, 415, 421, 441, 451, 490, 501, 542, 545f., 572f., 680, 851, 3350. We must, of course, say that Father, Son, and Spirit possess self-consciousness and that each one is aware of the two other "persons." But precisely this self-consciousness (as subjective, not as understood in its objectivity) comes from the divine essence, is common *as one* to the divine persons, is therefore a *moment* of the concrete person, so that he may be defined as "a distinct subject in a rational nature." But it is not a *constitutive* moment of the "person" as such, as distinct from the "essence" (nature), although it must be mentioned if we wish to explain the difference between a "hypostasis" with self-awareness and a subhuman thing-like "hypostasis." Cp. B. Lonergan, *op. cit.*, volume II, pp. 186–193.

"subjectivities" must be carefully kept away from the concept of person in the present context.[30]

In the third section we shall further consider that which follows from the above two paragraphs concerning the correct way of putting Father, Son, and Spirit as such, as different, under *one* word and *one* concept (as *conceptus vagus*).

D. Some Consequences for a Deeper Understanding

Textbook theology may draw from this doctrine of the Church the following immediate consequences.[31]

1. COMMON ACTIVITY "AD EXTRA" AND APPROPRIATION

Inasmuch as an "activity *ad extra*" (hence the creation of finite reality as distinct from God) is based upon the omnipotence of the one Godhead (upon the divine essence), there is only one outward activity of God, exerted and possessed as one and the same by Father, Son, and Spirit, according to the peculiar way in which each of them possesses the Godhead (DS 415, 441, 501, 531, 542, 545f.). Hence when such kind of activity is, in ecclesiastical usage, attributed by preference to one of the divine persons, it is also implicitly attributed to both other persons and *in this sense* only "appropriated" to the one person. The reason for this preference lies in a certain "affinity" of this outward activity with the peculiar nature of the divine person in question (DS

---

30. Hence within the Trinity there is no reciprocal "Thou." The Son is the Father's self-utterance which should not in its turn be conceived as "uttering," and the Spirit is the "gift" which does not give in its turn. Jn. 17, 21; Gal. 4, 6; Rom. 8, 15 presuppose a *creaturely* starting point for the "Thou" addressed to the Father. Cp. B. Lonergan, *ibid.*, p. 196.

31. We shall note in what follows whether the official doctrine of the Church contains any of the points that we are making.

573, 3326). Hence there certainly are appropriated statements (cp. DS B 2). This, however, does not exclude two points:

(a) The activity which is common to all three persons and appropriated only to one is (as with the divine essence) possessed by each of the three persons in his own proper way. The threefold way of subsisting of this activity (considered *principiative*) is as intrinsic and necessary for its existence as it is necessary and essential for the divine essence to subsist as threefold. This implies, beyond the "affinity," a very essential factual content which is very often overlooked.[32]

(b) The existence of mere appropriations does not imply that God's "outward" relation can exist only in a way which is common to all three persons, as a single relation which can only be appropriated to one determined person. The axiom is absolutely valid only where the "supreme efficient cause" is concerned (DS 3814). Not-appropriated relations of a single person are possible when we have to do, not with an efficient causality, but with a quasi-formal self-communication of God,[33] which implies that each divine person possesses its own proper relation to some created reality.

2. NOTIONAL AND ESSENTIAL REALITIES AND STATEMENTS

In accordance with the distinction of Father, Son, and Spirit and with the identity of the one divine essence, which these three are, we may distinguish between "essential" and "notional" realities or statements. "Essential" is all that which is given

32. Bonaventure had clearly seen this. Cp. A. Gerken, *Theologie des Wortes*, 36f., 87f. Hence we may well ask whether the δὶ οὗ (through whom) which is stated about the Son as creator of the world (DS 40ff., 44, and so on) should be interpreted *only* as appropriation, or whether it does not also indicate the notional way in which the Son possesses the creative activity as communicated by the Father.

33. On this concept cp. the literature listed in our first chapter, notes 17 and 22.

with and stated with the divine essence. Such a statement may be made of God and of each divine person singly (God is Almighty, the Trinity is almighty, the Son is almighty). "Notional" is all that which refers to the persons in their distinction. Therefore, the following belong to the notional realities and statements.

(a) The *two processions* from the Father and from the Father through the Son, that is, the "begetting" of the Son as self-expression of the Father, and the one "spiration," the procession of the Spirit from the Father and from (and through) the Son as from the one principle of the Spirit.

(b) The *three person-constituting relations of origin*,[34] given with the processions, insofar as they imply relative opposition: the unoriginatedness (innascibility, unbegottenness, *Pater ingenitus*) of the Father as origin of the Son (Fatherhood), the origin through generation (utterance) from the Father (Sonship), both of these relations being identical with the *active* spiration of the Spirit by the Father and the Son; the origin of the Spirit from Father and Son (as opposed to the active "spiration").

(c) To these three person-constituting relations there must be added as notional reality the *fourth, not person-constituting relation:*[35] the active spiration of the Spirit as common peculiarity of Father and Son. This peculiarity belongs to the Son as deriving from the Father.

Insofar as these four relations must be conceived as an active producing or as a "passive" being produced, we may say that there are in God four "notional" acts,[36] active and passive begetting, active and passive spiration.

(d) Insofar as the Fatherhood and the unoriginatedness of the Father may be distinguished, without overlooking the fact that the Father's unoriginatedness is his fatherhood and should not

34. Cp. B. Lonergan, *op. cit.*, volume II, pp. 123ff., 161ff.
35. *Ibid.*, pp. 116–127, 161ff.
36. *Ibid.*, pp. 182–185.

be conceived as previous to it, as constituting a person, *five* "notional" properties (ἰδίωμα, γνωριστικόν) may be distinguished: unoriginatedness, fatherhood, sonship, active spiration, being spirated.

(e) On account of the unity of the essence, of the processions and of the relative oppositions, which constitute the persons, we speak of a mutual inexistence of the three persons (circumincession, circuminsession, περιχώρησις). The Son is from all eternity in the Father and the Father is from all eternity in the Son, and so on (DS 112f., 115, 1331).[37]

37. *Ibid.*, pp. 205ff.

III. A SYSTEMATIC OUTLINE
OF TRINITARIAN THEOLOGY

A. The Meaning and Purpose of the Submitted Essay

At this point an attempt should be made to propose a "systematic" doctrine of the Trinity. "Systematic" means here something very simple. After we have in great detail and patiently—considering the space available in a textbook—*heard* what Scripture, the history of dogma, and the official doctrine of the Church tell us about the Trinity, we must now *say* once more what we have heard. These two are not the same. It is not possible to hear in the same way everything which is said, to consider it equally important and significant. When one listens, there are always a few things that one does not hear. That is why saying what one *hears* and *saying* what one has heard and retained are not the same. Hence many things which we have or might have heard will not be said here. The reason is not merely lack of space or time. It has nothing to do with any contempt for earlier theology. Formerly it was quite legitimate to treat such questions as: Is the concept of relation in the Trinity connected more with the concept of a categorical or with that of a transcendental relation?[1] Is the purely mental distinction between essence and person in the Godhead a *virtualis distinctio rationis ratiocinatae* or a *distinctio formalis ex natura rei*, and so on?[2] Are the relations in God strictly as relations (as *esse ad*) a "perfection" or are they not?[3] How do

1. See the subtle explanations in B. Lonergan, *De Deo Trino*, volume II, pp. 291–315.
2. *Ibid.*, pp. 146ff.
3. *Ibid.*, pp. 143f., 208ff.

"relation" and "procession" conceptually (as person-constituting) stand to one another? What is the distinction between a *processio* (*per modum*) *operati* and a *processio* (*per modum*) *operationis* and which of the two may be applied to the Trinity?[4] One *may* consider these problems, and nobody is forbidden to do so. But must we treat such questions here, when, within the space allotted, other questions may seem more important—questions which are not explicitly mentioned in traditional school theology?

If we wished to explain *explicitly* why these problems no longer command our interest, we would have to enter into them so thoroughly that the purpose of such an explanation—to save time and space for other problems and for a suitable understanding of the Trinity—would again be sacrificed. Thus we can only state that we allow ourselves the same liberty which textbook theology has hitherto implicitly allowed itself, the liberty of selecting one's own themes. We take it for granted that many subtle considerations of school theology do not approach much nearer to the most secret, the ultimately forbidden goal: to render the mystery logically transparent and intelligible, by trying to master the formal dialectics of unity and trinity with increasingly sublime considerations. We take it for granted that modern man does not find it especially difficult (and rightly so, although other epochs and mentalities may feel differently about this) to know from the start that there may be statements, deriving from sources that remain distinct, which no longer allow of a *positive* synthesis (as opposed to a merely verbal one) and which may nevertheless stand very solidly in spite of the impossibility of such a synthesis. This allows us to indulge today in fewer metaphysical subtleties than previous school theology used to propose.[5]

4. *Ibid.*, pp. 79ff., 182f.
5. For these questions we refer explicitly to the standard textbooks of P. Galtier, A. d'Alès, A. Stolz, H. Dondaine, R. Garrigou-Lagrange, M.

The very purpose of this chapter explains why some repetition of what has been said in the two previous chapters is unavoidable and even necessary. Nor do we claim that what we say here takes up the doctrine of the Church *in such a way* that all of it would have been adequately elaborated. All ecclesiastical utterances, each according to its degree of binding authority, are, of course, valid and constitute a part of the systematic doctrine of the Trinity, even though several of them are not again clearly reiterated here.

B. *Developing the Starting Point*

What we have already proposed as the basic axiom of trinitarian theology will be our starting point here.

I. THE NECESSITY OF A "SYSTEMATIC" CONCEPTION OF THE "ECONOMIC" TRINITY

We cannot, however, be content with what has been said above about this starting point. We must now explain *more precisely what* is properly meant by this "economic" Trinity which is supposed to be the "immanent" Trinity. Of course, we have a provisional understanding of what is meant by "economic" Trinity. Salvation history, our experience of it, its biblical expression give us such a previous knowledge which remains forever the foundation and the inexhaustible, ever richer starting point, even after it has been systematized. It is precisely this previous knowledge which is really developed in detail in Christology and in the

---

Schmaus, J. Brinktrine, L. Billot, J. M. Dalmau, but especially to the very complete two volumes of B. Lonergan, *De Deo Trino*, although this very subtle work makes one aware of the limitations of such endeavors.

doctrine of grace. But it is not always evident that this is done in a way which suffices for our present purpose. Thus, even if we overlook the question whether it is theologically quite justified to treat the doctrine of the Trinity *before* Christology and the doctrine of grace, this previous knowledge of the economic Trinity, derived from salvation history and from the Bible, cannot simply be presupposed here. Nor can it really be exposed according to the methods of *biblical theology*. Hence the only method which remains is to make the bold attempt to conceptualize it here in a short systematic presentation. This attempt may be questionable, but there is no way of avoiding it. For though it is impossible to expose the whole experience of Bible and salvation history (that is, the whole of Christology and of the doctrine of grace), yet we may not simply bypass it. Moreover, it should be formulated, that is, systematically conceptualized, in such a way that it may help us immediately to express theologically the "immanent Trinity," our real theme. We have unavoidably already alluded several times to this "systematic" conception of the "economic Trinity," but only in hints and anticipations. We must now propose it in more detail.

2. THE INNER RELATION BETWEEN THE WAYS OF GOD'S SELF-COMMUNICATION

(*a*) When treating of the economic Trinity, we are concerned with the two distinct yet related ways (they determiné each other, yet they constitute a $\tau\acute{\alpha}\xi\iota s$)* of the free gratuitous self-communication of God to the spiritual creature in Jesus Christ and in the "Spirit." We say: "of God," and we do not presuppose thereby a "Latin" theology of the Trinity (as contrasted with the

---

* That is, there is a certain relation of priority and posteriority between the two of them. The Spirit cannot come before the Son. —Translator.

Greek one), but the biblical theology of the Trinity (hence, in a sense, the Greek one). Here God is the "Father," that is, the simply unoriginate God, who is always known as presupposed, who communicates *himself* precisely when and because his self-communication does not simply coincide with him in lifeless identity. In this self-communication he stays the one who is free, incomprehensible—in a word, unoriginate.

God's unoriginatedness, as manifested in his self-communication, possesses a positive character: the fact that the divine unoriginate communicates himself in no way threatens or impairs his absolute integrity.[6]

(*b*) Thus far there is no special problem, insofar as we presuppose the strict concept of God's self-communication which transcends the communication of a creature. The decisive question with respect to this concept is how it can help us understand the two ways of self-communication through the "Son" and the "Spirit." How can these two ways be understood as moments, innerly related to each other, yet distinct from one another, of the *one*

6. One might object that in fact we are concerned here with an essential unoriginatedness of the Father, hence practically with aseity. Yet it sounds as if the notional unoriginatedness of the Father were intended. This objection rests on a misunderstanding. In the self-communication of God, which does not let the communication lifelessly coincide with the communicator (this has still to be shown), the essence of unoriginatedness shows itself in its concreteness: divinity (aseity) which can communicate itself without thereby losing itself, yet without ultimately merely keeping to itself, for this would do away with the character of a *self*-communication. Hereby we refer concretely to the "person" of the Father, who is not only "fatherhood" (hence "notionality"), but the concrete God in the unity of essential aseity and notional fatherhood, concrete unoriginatedness. Should one say that something similar may be said also of Son and Spirit, we reply that it is true of them *as* communicated, insofar as they themselves are constituted by the fatherly self-communication. In other words, we can never conceive of a divinity which does not exist either as that of the Father or of the Son or of the Spirit.

self-communication of God, in such a way that the distinction too may really be brought under a "concept"?[7]

(c) It cannot be said that Catholic theology is clearly aware of this problem. It accepts the incarnation and the descent of the Spirit as two facticities connected by a rather extrinsic bond. Implicitly, it is convinced that the Spirit might well exist without the incarnation, that each divine person might become man, hence the Father too and the Spirit himself, that there might be an incarnation of the Logos (even with a soteriological purpose, such as of "condign satisfaction") which would not already in principle imply the descent of the Spirit. Thus these two self-communications of God are connected only by the bond of a moral decree of God. They can no longer be really understood as the inner, mutually related moments of the one self-communication, through which God (the Father) communicates himself to the world unto absolute proximity.[8] It follows that the difference between the incarnation and the descent of the Spirit, insofar as both of them are soteriological realities, is not clear. As long as one admits, for instance, that the Spirit could as well have become man and have assumed the "hypostatic function" with respect to Jesus' human "nature," there can be nothing in the incarnation (except for different words of Jesus) which would not also have been given

7. We do not have to explain in detail that such a (let us call it transcendental) question already presupposes the knowledge of the Son and the Spirit derived from salvation history. It does not claim to deduce them from our mere concept of a self-communication of God which we might perhaps abstractly construct without this experience. Yet such a question is not superfluous when the experience of the incarnation and the descent of the Spirit are already presupposed. There is a strange overlapping of experience and insight in transcendental necessity. Even that which is known only through factual experience may occasionally be recognized as necessary: thus, in the present case, the two moments of a freely posited reality, as belonging necessarily together.

8. We might note in passing that such mere facticity makes the incarnation smack of mythology.

in this other eventuality. As long as one presupposes that the communication of the Spirit is possible also without incarnation, nothing can be given by this descent of the Spirit as such which would make it essentially different from the incarnation of the Logos, except precisely the fact that, in the latter case, the Logos exercises the "hypostatic function" which could equally well have been assumed by the Spirit.

(*d*) That is why we start from the opposite assumption. We suppose that, when God freely steps outside of himself in *self*-communication (not merely through creation, positing other realities which are not himself), it is and must be the Son who appears historically in the flesh as man. And it is and must be the Spirit who brings about the acceptance by the world (as creation) in faith, hope and love of this self-communication. Insofar as this one self-communication of God, which occurs necessarily in these two complementary aspects, is *free*, the incarnation and the descent of God's Spirit are free, even though the connection between these two moments is necessary. At any rate, no solid dogmatic reason can be found in the official doctrine of the Church against this assumption. We have already said that it agrees with the pre-Augustinian tradition. *For us*, the reason why *we* prefer it is because, as we said briefly in Chapter I, otherwise it is impossible to reach an understanding of the doctrine of grace and of Christology. The fact that it is precisely the Logos who became man and the Spirit who "sanctifies" is a free event, if and because God's self-communication is free. If, on the other hand, we presuppose this event and even then consider the incarnation of the Logos as "free," and the sanctification by the Spirit[9] as

9. Should someone say that sanctification is merely "appropriated" to the Spirit, we would reply: first, *gratis asseritur, gratis negatur* (a gratuitous affirmation, which we reject without proof); secondly, given the incarnation, this objection loses all sense.

"free," then salvation history itself tells us nothing anymore
about the Father, the Son, and the Spirit. The doctrine of the
Trinity turns into a verbal accompaniment of a salvation history
which in itself would for us (without this "for us" it is no longer
salvation history) be absolutely unchanged if the Father or the
Spirit had become man.

(e) Hence the question can only be how the incarnation and
the descent of the Spirit can, in the properties we know about
them through revelation, be so "conceptualized" [auf den
"Begriff gebracht"], or understood that they look like moments
of the one self-communication of God, hence as one economic
Trinity, and not merely as two "functions" of two divine
hypostases, which might be exchanged at will.

Formulated in this way, the question is difficult to answer,
especially since we cannot here collect, develop, and discuss the
many hints which are scattered over countless places in biblical
and theological tradition. Hence we can only make an attempt,
which amounts to a beginning. It is justified by the fact that it
must unavoidably be made if in the present climate of opinion
we are to overcome the strange suspicion that the Trinity belongs
to mythology.

3. A FORMAL EXPOSITION OF THE CONCEPT
OF "GOD'S SELF-COMMUNICATION"

We presuppose the existence of God, and we keep in mind that
every knowledge of God, however conceived and theologically
interpreted, brings up the question of God's relation to us, thus
implying the concept of a self-communication of God at least
as an asymptotic boundary concept of this relation. In such a
context and remembering what we have said above, "God's self-
communication" is not a concept which must necessarily arouse

the suspicion of mythology; on the other hand, far from excluding the "mystery," it includes it. Hence it is theologically unobjectionable.[10]

Once we presuppose this concept of the self-communication of God, it reveals to us a fourfold group of aspects:[11] (a) Origin–Future; (b) History–Transcendence; (c) Invitation–Acceptance; (d) Knowledge–Love.

We must first explain each of these double aspects. Next we must consider the inner unity of the first members of every pairing as contrasted with that of the second members. If we succeed in this second task, we shall understand that the one self-communication of God occurs in *two* basic ways which belong together.

4. SELF-COMMUNICATION TO A PERSONAL RECIPIENT

Of course, these four basic aspects of God's self-communication appear to us first from *our* point of view, from the point of view of *our* conditions as *creatures and as men*. There are two reasons why this should not arouse any suspicion of modalism.

First, we are speaking of self-*communication*. Hence the concept of the "addressee" can never be excluded. The mystery of

10. The concept of self-communication means: (a) the absolute nearness of God as the incomprehensible mystery which remains forever such; (b) the absolute freedom, hence the irreducible facticity of this self-communication, which remains a "mystery" for this reason too; (c) that the inner possibility of the self-communication as such (absolute communication of the absolutely incomprehensible) can never be perceived. It is experienced as an event in pure facticity, it cannot be deduced from another point, and as such again it remains a mystery.

11. We do not claim here and in what follows that we can necessarily distinguish *only* these four couples of aspects. It suffices that they exist and that, in the unity of all the elements of either side, they sufficiently clarify for us the doubleness of God's self-communication.

God's self-communication consists precisely in the fact that God really arrives at man, really enters into man's situation, assumes it himself, and *thus* is what he is. Being and remaining what he thus is, he really arrives, and the situation of the addressee is not an *a priori* obstacle to his arriving. Not so with animals. Their nature renders it apriorily impossible that a word *remains* a *human* word and does not turn, when addressed to them, into an animal signal.

In the second place (once more a double consideration): creation as it is must or may, without detracting from the unity of the creative "outward" activity of the one God, be considered as a moment of God's self-communication. It is the condition of the possibility of constituting an addressee. This is true even if, "in itself," creation might have occurred without such a self-communication. Now Christ's "human nature" is not something which happens to be there, among many other things, which might equally well have been hypostatically assumed, but it is precisely that which comes into being when God's Logos "utters" himself outwards. Hence if we postulate these four double aspects of a self-communication of God first "from below," from our point of view, this does not necessarily imply that we add something to this self-communication, which would be extrinsic to it in itself, insofar as it comes from God. These structures of the world and of the person may be conceived as the reality which, although distinct from God, comes into being precisely when and insofar as God presupposes, as a condition of its possibility, the addressee of his self-communication.

The self-communication of the free personal God who gives himself as a person (in the modern sense of the word!) presupposes a personal recipient. It does not just happen that God communicates himself to him; the addressee of the self-communication must be such on account of the very nature of this self-communication. If God wishes to step freely outside of himself, he must create man. There is no need to explain in detail that he must then create a spiritual-personal being, the only one who possesses the "obediential potency" for the reception of such a self-communication.

The only question which traditional school theology might raise is the objection that an immaterial, uncorporeal personal subject (an "angel," therefore) must be considered as another possible addressee of God's self-communication; that, in fact, there are angels who have received this self-communication. It is impossible to refute this objection completely here. But it should not be considered valid. In order to see this we must first show that there exists a unity of spirit and matter (the world), in which the angels too remain included in their own way; that the grace of the angels is also the grace of Christ, hence a moment of this self-communication of God which proceeds towards the one world, as constituted of spirit and matter, the latter being the necessary otherness of the finite spirit. While this self-communication is free, it necessarily finds, in the incarnation (and in no other way), its peak and irreversible finality. In this one process the angels receive grace as peculiar personal moments in the one world of spirit and matter.

If we think along these lines the above objection disappears without need of further explanation.[12] At any rate, a really Christian angelology must, from the start, fit in with the fact of the God-*man*. It should not start from the hypothesis or implication that God might equally well have become an angel, if only he had wished it. For whether we like it or not, such a hypothesis makes of the incarnation an unbelievable myth; it does not let God himself appear in the flesh; that which appears no longer expresses anything of the one who appears.

12. Cp. K. Rahner, "Angelologie," in *Lexikon für Theologie und Kirche*, volume I, pp. 534–538.

5.   TOWARDS A BETTER UNDERSTANDING
OF THE SINGLE BASIC ASPECTS OF THE SELF-COMMUNICATION

The four double aspects thus become intelligible under this assumption, namely, that the human personal subject is the addressee who is, of his very nature, demanded by the divine self-communication, which creates him as the condition of its own possibility. Let us now consider each of these aspects separately.

In agreement with the nature of the addressee this communication as communicated (but as still going on) has an *origin* and a *future* (the *first* couple of aspects), in the open tension between both moments: a beginning, in which the addressee of a possible divine self-communication is constituted by the will which decided this self-communication. This beginning or origin aims at a future (the total communication of God), which should not be considered as that which develops naturally from the beginning, but as something which, despite the latter's finalization towards the future, stands opposed to the beginning as the other moment of something radically new, something separated by a real history of freedom. This *first* couple of aspects should be sufficiently intelligible if we keep in mind the freedom of the communication and the historicity of the addressee.

History and *transcendence* are the *second* couple of aspects under which God's self-communication comes, if it wishes to reach the *whole* of man, since in it God as origin of man gives himself wholly and immediately unto salvation. It cannot be our task to develop here the meaning of these two concepts with philosophical precision and thoroughness. But even so we may understand that there belongs to man essentially the following open difference which we indicate with these two words: the difference (in knowledge and in action) between the concrete object and the "horizon" within which this object comes to stand, between the *apriori* and the *aposteriori* of knowledge and freedom, between the way in which knowledge and activity reach the well-determined concrete here and now (*so* and *not* otherwise) and the open range which knowledge and action anticipate, from whose vantage point, by limiting themselves, they establish the "object," while ever again discovering its contingency. This distinction does not imply that only the horizon, the unlimited whereunto of transcendence and transcendence itself, are what count, whereas the object would only be that which mediates the experience of transcendence, something which must disappear at the end. Transcendence and its whereunto have their history in the object itself. And it is the unity of these two elements, as it brings about distinction, which refers to God. Neither of the two moments alone should be made God's substitute. We maintain, against any kind of "imageless" mysticism of an experience of transcendence in the mere anonymity of the mystery, that transcendence is seen and found in the object itself. The latter is itself only as it offers itself in the open space of transcendence, which co-constitutes the object because it does not identify itself with it in lifeless identity. We do not have to study here the more precise relation between transcendence and openness to the future. At any rate we may say: if there occurs a self-communication of God to historical man, who is still becoming, it can occur only in this unifying duality of history and transcendence which man is.

If man is the being with the one duality of origin and future, if he is history in (into) transcendence, and *thus* the free being, then God's self-communication must also mean the difference between *offer* and *acceptance* (the *third* couple of aspects) of this self-communication. We do not deny thereby but rather affirm that the very acceptance of a divine self-communication through the power and act of freedom is one more moment of the self-communication of God, who gives himself in such a way that his self-donation is accepted in freedom.

The *fourth* couple of aspects seems at first to be of a quite different nature: *knowledge* and *love*, actuation of truth and actuation of love. Yet this double aspect too necessarily characterizes God's self-communication as such and in its totality. If we presuppose that knowledge ultimately terminates in bodily action and not merely in abstract thought, then that objection is at once overcome which claims that the actuation of truth (as original unity of practical and theoretical knowledge) is a regional-categorial and not a transcendental determination of man, which would not have to be considered, at least not at the start, if we wish to characterize God's self-communication, which is addressed to the *whole* of man as *such*.

On the other hand, this duality in man can neither be overcome nor completed. It *cannot be overcome*: for despite their "perichoresis," their transcendental unity (and a τάξις, which must not be considered here), "the true" and "the good," knowledge *and* love, are originally distinct, and neither can be understood as a *mere* moment of the other. Willing is neither the *mere* motor component of knowledge nor a mere "appetite" of an ultimate unique "good," which would be the "true." Nor is knowledge only the radiance of love, which would make of it a mere moment of love. This transcendental duality can also *not be completed* by further determinations, as for instance by some equally primordial "beautiful" or by "feeling" and so on. This is so not only because this would seriously endanger a real understanding of the intra-trinitarian processions, of which there necessarily can only be *two*, and thus make it impossible to maintain the basic axiom of the identity of "economic" and "immanent" Trinity. If we understand will, freedom, "good" in their true and total essence, that is, above all not only as a mere drive but as love for a person, a love which does not simply strive towards this person

93

but rests in his full goodness and "splendor," *then* we can see *no* reason for adding a third and higher power to this duality. Knowledge and love in their duality describe the reality of man. Hence a self-communication of God to man must present itself to man as a self-communication of absolute truth and absolute love.

6. THE INNER UNITY OF THE DIFFERENT ASPECTS OF GOD'S SELF-COMMUNICATION

If now we wish to place this one self-communication of God to man under one *theological* concept, we must explain why and how, if we take *either* side of the *four* couples of aspects, they may be understood as a *unity*. If this is possible, it follows that there are *two* and only two basic manners of the self-communication of God, which are distinct *and* condition each other in such a way that the specific character of each may be grasped conceptually and distinguished from the other.

(*a*) Regarding *some* of these aspects, the unity is easily understandable. Origin–history–offer clearly constitute a unity. The origin and history of all not-divine reality and its history is God's will, as it proffers divine self-communication; while the historic world is constituted as the addressee who may freely accept such self-communication. The offer of divine self-communication is the origin of the world and of history, the master plan according to which the world is projected. This beginning does not absorb the end as merely one of its explicative moments. For this beginning constitutes the future as something open and new, because, where the future is really understood as historic, and not merely as "evolutive," it is not pre-empted in the beginning.

In this connection we must keep in mind the following point. If the self-proffering of God to the world is a real offer, to *historic men*, then, it has taken place definitively and irrevocably only when it is historically *there* in the "absolute bringer of salvation," when the proffering of divine self-communication not only constitutes a world as the addressee of its offer, but posits itself irrevocably as historical. This too still belongs to the "beginning," to the origin of history, insofar as the latter is understood as the history of the acceptance of this offered self-communication. Elsewhere, in Christology, it should be explained that the historical "being-there" of the absolute and irrevocable self-offering is precisely what we theologically call the "incarnation of God," hence that the latter is implied in the concept of the "absolute bringer of salvation." The unity of the above mentioned moments should become clearer still when it is explicitly contrasted with the unity of the opposed moments (future–transcendence–acceptance).

(*b*) It is more difficult to see why *truth* as a moment of divine self-communication belongs on the side of the three moments whose unity we have shown above. Why does truth or knowledge originally belong more on the side of these three moments (origin–history–offer) than on the side of the three opposed moments (future–transcendence–acceptance)? Why, for instance, does "truth" have a more primordial[13] affinity with history than love has? If we wish to get anywhere here we should not simply take for granted a popular conception of truth and knowledge which comes from the Greeks. Truth is not first the correct grasping of a state of affairs.[14] It consists first in letting our own personal essence

13. When studying these problems we must always note that the two basic aspects of the divine self-communication condition each other from the start. Hence we *must* be able to show that moments of one basic manner of self-communication must also have meaning and importance for the other one. This explains why the "appropriations" seem to shift arbitrarily. Hence we are concerned with the question of the *more original* connection of one such moment (for instance, of "truth") with either basic aspect.

14. Although secondarily this too is correct. Even when we know a state

come to the fore, positing ourself without dissimulation, accepting ourself and letting this authentic nature come to the fore in truth also in the presence of others. No doubt, as we reveal our genuine nature, there is (as act) a voluntary moment, but the latter is still an inner moment of truth itself. This true "revealing"—letting our nature come to the fore in the presence of others—is (when it includes a free commitment to the other) what we call "fidelity." Hence truth is first the truth which we *do*, the deed in which we firmly posit ourself for ourself and for others, the deed which waits to see how it will be received. This helps us understand that the process of self-communication, insofar as it constitutes itself as origin, history, and offer, shows itself as *truth*. Divine self-communication, as a "revelation" of God's nature, is truth for us. It occurs as faithful offer, and in this way it posits a beginning and becomes definitely established in the concreteness of history. Looking at it from the other side, we may say: when God's self-communication as beginning and history is still given as offer, it also appears as faithful truth, and it turns into history. Yet, as such, it is not yet *the* promise which has already penetrated into the addressee, has been accepted by him, *becoming* love and *begetting* love in him. And if it is to elicit the answer of *free* love in man's decision, this self-communication must render such an answer possible, make room for it, be faithful to itself, proffer itself by way of objective presentation, that is, by way of truth.

(c) It is not so easy to see the *unity* of the *four* opposed moments: future–transcendence–acceptance–love. It is relatively easy to understand the unity of future and transcendence. It suffices to realize that the future does not merely mean that which is still

---

of affairs, truth is given only in the judgment. But the judgment is the act by which the state of affairs is allowed to come to the fore as a determination of the environment or of the world of the subject himself. Hence it is also a partial aspect of the process by which the subject lets his own (concrete) nature come to the fore and accepts it in fidelity.

to come, but as a modality of God's self-communication it means "God" insofar as, communicated and accepted, he gives himself to man as the latter's consummation. *For this reason* it must open the field of transcendence or even contain transcendence within itself as its own moment.[15] Transcendence arises where God gives himself as the future. By transcendence we mean both transcendence as openness for a *possible* absolute future, *in case* this future should become available (the "natural" transcendentality of the spirit), and also transcendence deriving from grace as the possibility of accepting an absolute future which is in fact presented.[16]

Insofar as the self-communication must be understood as *absolutely* willed by God it must carry its acceptance with it. If we are not to downgrade this communication to the level of a human *a priori* and thus do away with it, the acceptance must be brought about by the self-communicating God himself. The freedom of the acceptance as a power *and* also as an act must be conceived as posited by God's creative power, without in any way impairing the nature of freedom. Insofar as the divine self-communication implies the will of its acceptance, it constitutes transcendence and the future, and the arrival of the absolute future itself which carries their acceptance with it. It is more difficult to explain how the divine self-communication, insofar as it thus constitutes transcendence-futurity-acceptance of the future, must be characterized as love. Yet the self-communication which wills itself abso-

15. We do not have to examine these two possibilities in more detail. We might understand "transcendence" as "man's futurity," openness, finalization towards the future. Hence the *future* would be connected with transcendence, yet mean more than it: the having-come-to-pass of the real future, which, as the absolutely new, is neither simply identical with futurity (or deducible from it alone), nor simply that which is to come later and is not yet, but that which, as such, in its coming constitutes the concrete man of "hope," who "possesses" already as "not yet given" that which is still to come.

16. On the concept of "absolute future," cp. K. Rahner, *Schriften zur Theologie*, volume VI, pp. 77–88.

lutely and creates the possibility of its acceptance and this acceptance itself, is precisely what is meant by love. It is the specifically divine "case" of love, because it creates its own acceptance and because this love is the freely offered and accepted self-communication of the "person."

7. THE TWO FUNDAMENTAL MODALITIES
OF DIVINE SELF-COMMUNICATION

Hence the divine self-communication possesses two basic modalities: self-communication as truth and as love. This looks at first like a very simple result of the previous considerations; yet, in their light, the statement implies that this self-communication, insofar as it occurs as "truth," happens in history; and that insofar as it happens as love, it opens this history in transcendence towards the absolute future. This is not evident at once. History as concrete, in which the irrevocability of the divine self-communication is made apparent, and transcendence towards the absolute future, are opposites, and as such they keep the one divine self-communication separated in their modalities. But this historic manifestation as truth can be perceived only in the horizon of transcendence towards God's absolute future; this absolute future is irrevocably promised as love by the fact that this promise is established in concrete history (of the "absolute bringer of salvation"). Insofar as these two statements are true, the two modalities of divine self-communication are not separated, nor are they tied together simply by divine decree. They constitute the one divine self-communication which assumes the form of truth in history, of origin and offer, of love in transcendence towards the freely accepted absolute future.

Suppose we wish to put these two basic modalities under one short formula. Let us make "history" stand for one side of the four couples of aspects, and "spirit" for the other (it is easy to understand why the latter word was chosen rather than one of the four aspects of that side). Then we may say: *the divine self-communication occurs in unity and distinction in history (of the truth) and in the spirit (of love).*

Both basic modalities condition one another. They derive from the nature of the self-communication of the unoriginate God who remains incomprehensible, whose self-communication remains a mystery both as possible and as actual. But the two modalities are not simply the same thing.

C. Transition from "Economic" to "Immanent" Trinity

Thus we may have succeeded in some way in conceptualizing the "economic" Trinity. The question arises now whether, with our concept of the "economic" Trinity, we have also practically been speaking of what in the Church's statements about the Trinity is meant by Father, Son, and Spirit, hence of the "immanent" Trinity. In the first section we have already said all the essential about the basic axiom of the identity of the "economic" and the "immanent" Trinity. But now the question arises whether the concept we have developed of the "economic" Trinity allows us to postulate not only some kind of "immanent" Trinity, but the Trinity acknowledged in the official declarations of the Church.[17]

First, appealing to the above mentioned basic axiom, we may say: the differentiation of the self-communication of God in

17. In order to evaluate correctly the way we answer this question, we must also keep in mind what will have to be said later about the suitability and the questionability of the concept of "person" in the doctrine of the Trinity.

history (of truth) and spirit (of love) must belong to God "in himself," or otherwise this difference, which undoubtedly exists, would do away with God's *self*-communication.[18] For these modalities and their differentiation either are in God himself (although we first experience them from our point of view), or they exist only in us, they belong only to the realm of creatures as effects of the divine creative activity. But then they are God's mediations in that difference which lies between creator and that which is created out of nothing. Then they can only be that communication of God which occurs precisely in creation, in which what is created contains a transcendental reference to the God who remains forever beyond this difference, thus at once "giving" him and withdrawing him. Hence there occurs no self-communication, God himself is not there, he is only represented by the creature and its transcendental reference to God. Of course, the real self-communication of God too has its effect in the creature[19] (the creaturely reality of Christ and "created" grace); and the relation between self-communication as such (divine hypostasis as hypostatically united; uncreated grace) and the effect in the creatures may ontologically be explained as one

18. This is not a rationalistic *a priori* "proof" of the existence of the "immanent" Trinity. For this statement already presupposes this self-communication as testified by revelation and as a mystery. Moreover, we have already noted above that our outline of the modalities of God's self-communication is already guided by the facts of the incarnation and of the communication of God's Spirit, facts which we know from the history of revelation. Between *a priori* deduction and a merely *a posteriori* gathering of random facts, there exists a middle way: the recognition of what is experienced aposteriorily as transcendentally necessary, because it has to be, because it cannot be mere facticity, whatever the reasons from which this necessity may be inferred. When this necessity is formally grasped, we are allowed to try to understand it, to the best of our ability, from that which is known aposteriorily. This way of knowing the "necessary" is frequently used, for example, by St. Thomas.

19. Such an effect may also be indispensable for the constitution of the self-communication, for its real arriving among us, as may be shown by Christology and by the polemics of medieval theology against the doctrine of grace of Peter Lombard.

prefers, according to the different theories which exist about this point in Christology and the doctrine of grace. But if there is to be a real self-communication and not mere creation, this creaturely reality is, at any rate, not mediating in the sense of some substitute, but as a consequence of the self-communication (and as a previous condition brought about by itself). God's self-communication, as concretely *experienced* by us, may always already imply this creaturely consequence and condition. But if this created reality were the real mediation of the self-communication by way of substitute, in the difference between creator and creature, there would no longer be any *self*-communication. God would be the "giver," not the *gift itself*, he would "give himself" only to the extent that he communicates a gift distinct from himself. The creaturely difference which is experienced also in the case of God's self-communication ("humanity of Christ," "created grace") does not constitute the difference of both modalities of the divine self-communication but allows this difference to appear as the consequence of this self-communication.

D. How the "Economic" Trinity Is Grounded in the "Immanent" Trinity

When from this point of view we try to express the "economic" Trinity, as "immanent," that is, as it is in God, prescinding from his free self-communication, we may say what follows:[20]

(*a*) There is real difference in God as he is in himself between one and the same God insofar as he is—at once and necessarily—

20. We consciously give up here the explicit use of the concept of "person" for two reasons: first because we have presented the "economic" Trinity without using this word, so that our basic axiom does not (yet) urge us to use it; and because we shall presently have to discuss explicitly the use of this concept in the doctrine of the Trinity.

the unoriginate who mediates himself to himself (Father), the one who is in truth uttered for himself (Son), and the one who is received and accepted in love for himself (Spirit)—and insofar as, *as a result of this*, he is the one who can freely communicate himself.[21]

(*b*) This real differentiation is constituted by a double self-communication of the Father, by which the Father communicates *himself*, while, as the one who utters and receives, he posits, precisely through this self-communication, his real distinction from the one who is uttered and from the one who is received. That which is communicated,[22] insofar as it makes the communication into an authentic self-communication, while not suppressing the real distinction between God as communicating and as communicated, may rightly be called the divinity, hence the "essence" of God.

(*c*) The bond between the original self-communicator and the one who is uttered and received,[23] a bond which implies a distinction, must be understood as "relative" (relational). This follows

21. We should not overlook the following logical connections: if the Trinity is necessary as "immanent," if God is absolutely "simple," and in fact freely communicates himself as "economic" Trinity, which *is* the "immanent" Trinity, then the "immanent" Trinity is the necessary condition of the possibility of God's free self-communication.

22. The use of the impersonal expression should be noted (the "neutral" article in the German text). We may distinguish between what is communicated, insofar as it includes the distinction between the one who utters himself, and the one who is uttered. In this case we think of the Son (the Logos). But we may also think of what is communicated as previous, as what makes the communication into a self-communication. In that case we are thinking of the essence.

23. In line with the peculiar nature of the "economic" Trinity, what is received must, of course, always be thought of as what, in being received by a loving welcome, is constituted as receivable, hence as distinct. In this statement under (*c*) we mean the one *who* is uttered and *who* is received, that is, that *which* is communicated, insofar as it subsists as distinct from that which communicates.

simply from the sameness of the "essence." This relationality should not be considered first of all as a means for solving apparent logical contradictions in the doctrine of the Trinity. As such a means, its usefulness is quite restricted. To the extent that relations are understood to be the most unreal of realities, they are less well suited to help us understand a Trinity which is most real. But relations are as absolutely *real* as other determinations; and an "apologetics" of the "immanent" Trinity should not start from the false assumption that a lifeless self-identity without any mediation is the most perfect way of being of the absolute existent. Afterwards it will then claim that in God the distinction is "only" relative, and thus try to remove the difficulty brought about by an assumption which amounted to a false initial conception of God's "simplicity."

E. The Problem of the Concept of "Person"

We shall now treat explicitly of the concept of person in the doctrine of the Trinity.[24] This is a question of terminology and of fact, and also one having a special importance for the systematization attempted here.

From the point of view of *terminology* the question is: is the concept of person suited to express faithfully that which is meant in connection with the doctrine of the Trinity? The question of *fact* is: what does the concept properly mean in *this* context? The question of importance for our *systematization heretofore presented* is: whether we have in this systematization arrived at the statement made by the official doctrine of the Church with the help of the concept of person. A clear-cut distinction between the three sub-questions is not too important.

24. Cp. above, pp. 26ff., 43ff., 56ff., 73ff.

I. FORMAL TERMINOLOGICAL DIFFICULTIES

Once again we must consider a few difficulties connected with the concept of person, especially as used in the doctrine of the Trinity. The mere fact that this concept is not used from the start in the doctrine of the Trinity (neither in the New Testament, nor among the early Fathers) is of itself not yet a matter of concern. Nevertheless, this fact allows us to adopt a critical position, and to state that a concept of this kind is, at any rate, not *absolutely* constitutive of our knowledge in faith about Father, Son, and Spirit as the one God. This faith can exist without reference to this concept. Moreover, *in the doctrine of the Trinity* this concept has aspects not found in any other concept ("individuality" and "distinction" excepted).[25] It attempts to generalize once more that which is absolutely unique. When we say: "there are three persons in God, God subsists in three persons" we generalize and add up something which cannot be added up,[26] since that which alone is really common to Father, Son, and Spirit is precisely the one and only Godhead, and since there is no higher point of view from which the three can be added *as* Father, Son, and Spirit. Wherever individuality and distinction exist in diverse realizations, it is possible to add up several of them without special difficulty, even when they are designated with different

25. What follows is, of course, a familiar and much discussed theme of classic theology. Cp., for instance, St. Thomas, I, q. 30, a. 3; a. 4. We presuppose St. Thomas's concept of the person as one which, better than the concept of the person of Boethius or of Richard of St. Victor, may be of use in the doctrine of the Trinity: *subsistens distinctum in natura rationali* (that which subsists as distinct in a rational nature).

26. One can, of course, say that these are "transcendental numbers," which do not mean a multiplicity (cp. Lonergan, *op. cit.*, volume II, p. 166), thus admitting that nothing is added up here, that the "threeness" consists in this, that *we* can and must predicate God three times, namely, of the Father, the Son, and the Spirit.

concepts (for example, three "individuals"). But this is precisely not the case here. Furthermore, "person" as a concrete concept, in contrast with "personality" ("subsistence," "subsistentiality"), means not formally the distinction as such, but those who are distinct. But ours is a case where we should speak of three persons, yet not think of three who are distinct as multiplied also in their essence, as we may do without any difficulty in other instances, e.g., when we speak of "three individuals."

This shows us already that, in reference to God, we may not speak of three persons in the same way that we do elsewhere. Hence the kerygmatic difficulty comes up ever again with new virulence: because of linguistic usage elsewhere, we keep forgetting that "three persons" means neither a group-building multiplication of the essence nor an "equality" of the personality of the three persons.

In the claim that, in God, "person" means an *individuum vagum* (a vague individual),[27] a concept is put forward which shows up the difficulty without solving it. The difficulty is one of linguistic usage which exists nowhere else. For if, in the creaturely (and philosophical) domain, we speak of "three" persons, we *directly* (*in recto*) intend by "person" (unless we suddenly correct our use of language under the influence of the doctrine of the Trinity) also his "rational nature." In such a context, nature is in fact multiplied, and we never discover in our experience a case where what "subsists as distinct" can be thought of as multiplied without a multiplication of natures. It should be admitted, moreover, that this difficulty occurs for all notional statements about the Trinity whenever numbers are used (for instance, the *two* processions).

At any rate, if we wish to understand the use of "three persons" correctly (this supposes that we forget the usual meaning of the

27. Thomas Aquinas, I, q. 30, a. 4; Lonergan, *op. cit.*, volume II, pp. 165f.

words), we must always return to the original experience of salvation history. Here we experience the Spirit, and we experience him as God (who is only one); we experience the Son, as God; and the Father, as God. When we generalize and say that we experience "three" persons, we do so subsequently to our experience. Our generalization is, *at least* at first, a logical explanation, not some new extra knowledge not included in the original experience. It serves only to remove a modalistic misunderstanding of our experience.

2. THE CONCEPT OF "PERSON" IN OFFICIAL STATEMENTS AND ITS OWN INDEPENDENT HISTORICAL DEVELOPMENT

Nonetheless, the main difficulty regarding the concept of person in the doctrine of the Trinity is rather different, and we have already mentioned it several times before now: when *today we* speak of person in the plural, we think almost necessarily, because of the modern meaning of the word,[28] of several spiritual centers of activity, of several subjectivities and liberties. But there are not three of these in God—not only because in God there is only *one* essence, hence *one* absolute self-presence, but also because there is only *one* self-utterance of the Father, the Logos. The Logos is not the one who utters, but the one who is uttered. And there is properly no *mutual* love between Father and Son, for this would presuppose two acts. But there is loving self-acceptance of the Father (and of the Son, because of the τάξις of knowledge and love), and this self-acceptance gives rise to the distinction. Of course, that which we call "three persons" in God exists in God with self-awareness. There is in God a knowledge of these three persons (hence in each person about himself and about the two

28. We shall have to say more about the *theological* meaning of this fact. Cp. below, pp. 115f., and note 29.

other persons), a knowledge about the Trinity both *as consciousness* and as *"object"* of knowledge (as known).[29] But there are
not three consciousnesses; rather, the one consciousness subsists
in a threefold way. There is only one real consciousness in God,
which is shared by Father, Son, and Spirit, by each in his own
proper way. Hence the threefold subsistence is not qualified by
three consciousnesses. The "subsistence" itself is as such not
"personal," if we understand this word in the modern sense. The
"distinctness" of the persons is not constituted by a distinctness
of conscious subjectivities, nor does it include the latter. This
distinctness is conscious. However, it is not conscious for three
subjectivities, but it is the awareness of this distinctness in one
only real consciousness.[30]

This difficulty is not overcome merely by defining the concept
of person in such a way that, as applied to God, it does not include this distinct "personality." For "person" should help us
understand what is meant in the present case, it should not be

29. In God all knowledge is original, there is in him no receptive knowledge nor (essentially) any difference between a subject conscious for himself and an object of this consciousness. Thus the Father expresses himself
by being self-present in knowledge without any difference, *by* being
"conscious" of himself, and not *in order to* know himself. Hence the
human difference between *being conscious* and *being known* (the subject's
self-presence in knowledge—the objective representation of that which is
known) does not apply to God. This does not mean, however, that in God
the three subjects have three different consciousnesses, through which they
are consciously self-present. Although we may say that each of the divine
"persons" is "conscious" of the two others, and does not merely possess
them as "objects" of knowledge, this derives not only from the identity of
the divine essence (and from the accompanying absolute self-presence of
this essence) in the Father, the Son, and the Spirit, but *also* from the fact
that every "notional act" (identical with the divine essence) renders, as
conscious (and relative), every other notional act co-conscious. In brief,
"thus we conclude that the three subjects are aware of each other through
one consciousness which is possessed in a different way by the three of
them" (Lonergan, *op. cit.*, volume II, p. 193).

30. This one consciousness would constitute one unique (absolute)
person only for somebody who, in this whole question, would again presuppose the modern concept of person and thus becloud the whole issue.

modified to conform to the thing that is meant, although a certain interaction between the concept imposed *from outside* upon the thing (to determine it) and the thing itself cannot be avoided. Such a concept does not, however, simply come under the power of the Church. It has a history which cannot be directed in an autonomous and autarchic way by the Church *alone*. When the magisterium and theology circumscribe a concept, they do not remove it from its history and evolution, at least not in fact, that is, for the understanding of concrete man, whose intellectual horizon and store of concepts is not autarchically "ecclesiastical." Hence the Church and its official proclamation stand ever again before a new task, because the fitness and intelligibility of a given concept with regard to a certain reality may change, and because the Church, which must speak as intelligibly as possible for concrete man, cannot prevent such change.

This applies also to the "concept of person." While formerly "person" meant directly (*in recto*) only the distinct subsistence, and co-signified the rational nature only indirectly (*in obliquo*)—according to the thing-like way of thinking of the Greeks—the "anthropocentric turn" of modern times requires that the spiritual-subjective element in the concept of person be first understood.[31] Hence the Church faces a situation that did not always exist. On the other hand, it is evident that the regulation of language, which is necessary in a Church as a community of a shared social worship and confession, cannot be undertaken by the single theologian at will. The only thing he can do at present

31. This started rather early, of course. Thus the dispute about monotheletism could not have brought up the question how two ἐνέργειαι (two conscious "centers of activity") are possible in the same person, if the concept of person had not already shown that tendency which, in modern times, has led to a conscious shift in its meaning. We cannot here enter into this extremely difficult problem, which has not yet been historically investigated in a satisfactory manner, which has not even been disentangled (neo-Platonism as a later form of classic philosophy; Christianity-(neo)-Platonism).

is *also* to use the concept of person in the doctrine of the Trinity, and to defend it, to the extent of his power, from misunderstandings that it is threatened by. The magisterium forbids him to suppress such concepts on his own authority, but also obliges him to work at their fuller explanation. This he can do only if he uses other words for the official ecclesiastical concepts which are to be explained. But if such an explanation is, in principle, legitimate, and even necessary, and if, in a concrete case, it is conducted correctly, then it cannot be basically unjustified that such an explanation take concrete shape and be summarized in some other concept. We are then allowed to use such an explanatory concept without repudiating the concept that it explains.

3. THE POSSIBILITY OF OTHER THEOLOGICAL WAYS OF EXPRESSION

This brings us finally to the main question of this chapter. What would such an explanatory concept be that would explain and correctly interpret the concept of "person"? Does it correctly and completely correspond to the concept that is to be explained?

In order to answer this question, and to summarize our previous considerations, we must (once more) start from our basic axiom. The one self-communication of the one God occurs in three different manners of given-ness, in which the one God is given concretely for us in himself, and not vicariously by other realities through their transcendental relation to God. God is the concrete God in each one of these manners of given-ness—which, of course, refer to each other relatively, without modalistically coinciding. If we translate this in terms of "immanent" Trinity, we may say: the one God subsists in three distinct manners of subsisting. "Distinct manner of subsisting" would then be the explanatory concept, not for person, which refers to that which subsists as distinct, but for the "personality" which makes God's concrete reality, as it meets us in different ways, into precisely this one who meets us *thus*. This meeting-us-thus must always be conceived as belonging to God in and for himself. The single "person" in God would then be: God as existing and meeting us in this determined distinct manner of subsisting.

The expression "distinct manner of subsisting" needs more explanation. We consider it better, simpler, and more in harmony with the traditional language of theology and the Church than the phrase suggested by Karl Barth: "manner of being."[32] First, if we prescind for a while from the word "manner," it says simply the same as the definition of "person" in Thomas: "that which subsists distinctly (in a rational nature),"[33] and the same as the corresponding Greek word.[34] What is meant by subsisting can become clear only in our own existence, where we encounter the concrete, irreducible, incommutable, and irreplaceable priority and finality of this experience. This-there is what subsists.[35] Thus our basic axiom is once more confirmed. Without our experience

32. Cp. K. Barth, *Church Dogmatics*, New York and London, n.d., volume I, part one, and *passim*.

33. Cp. Barth's analysis of the concept of person, *passim*.

34. In connection with this Greek word we should note that Eastern theology makes do with it alone and does not feel the need for the word πρόσωπον (person). This word is used when Eastern and Western theology are to be put in parallel. But it is not properly constitutive for Eastern theology. Moreover, ὑπόστασις is rather an abstract substantive, which refers to being *as* a distinct concrete something, hence precisely to the manner of subsisting.

35. This concrete real being-thus-and-not-otherwise in which experience sees a first *and* last datum has some peculiarities (for us, hence also in itself) when applied to the Trinity. Hence, in each instance (Father–Son–Spirit), (*a*) it points to another such being and entails it, although this other being remains permanently distinct from the first one; (*b*) the one who is *thus* is the same God who meets us and exists in another being-thus-and-not-otherwise. Hence he must be designated by a "proper noun," yet, wholly *unlike* what happens in the rest of our experience, this "proper noun" does not exclude that the reality which meets us thus, can, in strict identity with this "that which," meet us (and exist) also in another thus-and-not-otherwise.

of Father, Son, and Spirit in salvation history, we would ultimately be unable to conceive at all of their subsisting distinctly
as the one God.

It is more difficult to justify, in the above phrase, the word
"distinct *manner* of subsisting." In this respect several points
must be considered. If the divine person as such consists in a
"relation," and if all that which is "absolute" is strictly identical
in God, then the word "manner" should not give rise to any
fundamental objection. Why could we not call "relationality" a
"manner"? It is clear that we cannot classify this word in a
determined category of a finite being ("mode"). But this is
equally true for all concepts which are used in the classic doctrine
of the Trinity ("act," "procession," "emanation," and so forth).
Hence to avoid misunderstandings, we must say about the word
"manner" what must be said and is said about all other concepts
in this connection: that they are employed analogically, that they
should be understood beyond the table of categories, that they
mean no potentiality, and posit no real distinction (except when
meant with a relation of opposition), and so on. Of course, the
phrase "distinct manner of subsisting" entails also the delicate
problem of "vague individual," which we mentioned above in
connection with the concept of "person." The concrete, the absolute, unique concreteness is here made into an abstract concept, a
most abstract concept possessing a minimum of unity. But if, in
connection with the statements of faith and theology, we are not
simply content (as we cannot be) with merely speaking of Father,
Son, and Spirit and then of the one God, then this inconvenience
is unavoidable. But even so there are advantages in speaking of
the "distinct manner of subsisting" or of God in three distinct
manners of subsisting, rather than of person. "Three persons"
says nothing about the unity of these three persons, so that this
unity must be brought from outside to the word by which we
designate the three persons. Of itself, "manner" at least suggests
the possibility that the same God, as distinct in a threefold

manner, is concretely "three-personal," or, the other way around, that the "three-personality" co-signifies the unity of the same God.

We must keep in mind, however, that regarding the Trinity, "distinct *manner* of subsisting" should not be understood in such a way as if this "manner" were something subsequent, a "modality" without which the substantially real might also exist. The concrete Godhead is necessarily in these manners of subsisting. It is impossible, except through a merely conceptual abstraction, to conceive of a Godhead that would, as real, be previous to these manners. That is why the one God is Father, Son, and Spirit. But this misunderstanding occurs as easily and must expressly be avoided in the word "relation" or "procession." The word "manner" alone is not suspect. Although the expression "manner of subsisting" very clearly emphasizes God's unity and (unlike the modern, unavoidably burdened word "person") does not evoke the idea of three subjectivities in God, it does not imply a specifically Latin conception of the Trinity, as opposed to an Eastern one. For these "distinct manners of subsisting" should be seen as relative and standing in a determined τάξις to each other (Father, Son, and Spirit). The first manner of subsisting at once constitutes God as Father, as unoriginate principle of the divine self-communication and self-mediation. Hence no "God" should be conceived behind this first manner of subsisting, as previous to this distinct subsistence and having first to assume it.

We must grant that "distinct manner of subsisting" says very little about Father, Son, and Spirit as such and about their unity, that it is a quite formalistic concept. But is the same not true for the concept of "relation," and also for the concept of "person" as soon as we drop from it the modern notion of subjectivity (as *moment* of the "personality," of the "subsistence"), which would have to be multiplied together with the threeness of the persons? If we keep any modern connotation out of the concept of the person as such (in God!), then it says simply no more than "distinct subject." Compared with the word "personality," the expression "distinct manners of subsisting" has the advantage of not as easily insinuating as "three persons" the multiplication of the essence and of the subjectivity.

If, then, the phrase more clearly underlines God's unity and unicity (even though we speak of *three* manners of subsisting, but precisely as *manners*), there can be nothing wrong with this. Finally, we might also state that the phrase "distinct manners of subsisting" says nothing else than three distinct "substantialities" —a word against which the classic theology of the Trinity has certainly no objection, since that theology too realizes that the word "subsistence" ("hypostasis"), although abstract in itself, is used concretely, hence that the distinction between "subsistence" and "substantiality" cannot be wholly avoided.

4. CONCRETE CONFIRMATION OF THE NEW CONCEPT

Let us further test the usefulness of the expression "distinct manners of subsisting" (while here and now methodically avoiding the word "person") by formulating a few basic statements about the Trinity with the help of this concept. We may say, then, that:

—the one God subsists in three distinct manners of subsisting;[36]
—the manners of subsisting of Father, Son, and Spirit are distinct as relations of opposition; hence these "three" are not the same one;[37]

36. We should, of course, *not* say that he is distinct in three manners of subsisting (cp. DS 2697, 2830).

37. But they are the same *something* [*dasselbe*]. We prefer not to call it the same *someone* [*derselbe*] because the masculine qualifier [*dieser, derselbe*] should, in order to avoid confusion and false identifications, be reserved for the existent in his last incommutable concreteness, in which it occurs and exists. However, this restriction entails, in the present case,

—the Father, Son, and Spirit are the one God each in a different manner of subsisting and in this sense we may count "three" in God;

—God is "threefold" through his three manners of subsisting;[38]

—God as subsisting in a determined manner of subsisting (such as the Father) is "somebody else" [*ein anderer*] than God subsisting in another manner of subsisting, but he is not "something else" [*etwas anderes*];

—the manner of subsisting is distinct through its relative opposition to another one; it is real through its identity with the divine essence;

—the one and same divine essence subsists in each of the three distinct manners of subsisting;

—hence "he who"[39] subsists in one of such manners of subsisting is truly God.

If we consider these and similar formulations, which may be made with the help of the concept "distinct manners of subsisting," we may safely state that they say exactly as much as the formulation which uses the word "person." We have already said and must not repeat the advantages of the use of the concept "distinct manners of subsisting" as compared with the concept of "person" and what difficulties it entails. This concept, which

---

the inconvenience that it obscures the fact that here "the same something" is already the one subjectivity of the one Godhead, which, as freely encountering us, cannot be considered as thinglike.

38. When we say that "God" has three manners of subsistence, this formulation is handy because of the word "manner": one *has* a manner. Yet we should keep in mind that, in such a formulation, "God" is employed in the same way as when (classically) we say: God "has" three subsisting ones (= persons). We may say that God "has" three (formally abstract) manners of subsistence ("subsistentialities") even though no "God" is in "possession" of the three distinct subsisting ones. He *is* the three subsisting ones.

39. About this "he who" [*der*] we must say what we said above of "the same someone" [*derselbe*] and "this someone" [*dieser*]: it refers to the one who concretely occurs, but it implies no distinction and no multiplication in that *which* occurs and exists.

intends to be nothing more than an explanation of the concept of person as meant in the doctrine of the Trinity—an explanation which is legitimated by the truly Thomistic definition of the "person"—should not, as we said above, induce us to give up the use of the concept of person. But using it together with the concept of person may serve the purpose of overcoming the false opinion that what is meant by "person," especially within the doctrine of the Trinity, is clearly evident. He who starts with this false opinion may verbally protest to the contrary, may emphasize the mysterious character of the Trinity, may know of the logical difficulties in reconciling the three "persons" with God's unity. Despite all this he will have great trouble avoiding a *hidden* pre-reflective tritheism.

F. A Comparison with the Classic "Psychological" Doctrine

Finally, we must consider more explicitly the problem of the "psychological doctrine of the Trinity." It is not possible to treat it here systematically. Such an attempt to bring home to the intelligence of the faith an understanding of the threefold-distinct manner of subsisting of the one God by means of psychological categories and according to the model of the spiritual self-actuation of man differs considerably from the method used in the present essay.[40] We shall confine ourselves to the following points.

I. THE POSSIBILITY OF SUCH AN ANALOGY

There can be no doubt about the basic justification of this attempt. But we must keep in mind that we are concerned here with

40. Cp. *Mysterium Salutis*, vol. II, pp. 157ff., 202ff., 211ff.

theological considerations (*theologoumena*), not with a doctrine imposed by the Church. We must, and rightly so, think of God as of a spirit; there can be nothing objectively real in God which is not also most formally spirit, self-presence, knowledge, and love. It follows that the threefold distinct manner of subsisting of the one God must have something to do with God's "spirituality," even if we cannot further clarify this connection. Moreover, an authentic metaphysics of the spirit tells us that there are two (and only two!) basic activities of the spirit: knowledge and love. On the other hand, in harmony with the threefold distinct manner of subsisting of the one God, we know of two (and only two!) processions or emanations within God, or, as we said, of two aspects of one divine self-communication which condition one another in a certain τάξις. We are allowed, then, to combine these two data and to connect, in a special and specific way, the intra-divine procession of the Logos from the Father with God's knowledge, and the procession of the Spirit from the Father through the Son with God's love.

This is justified, even though the statements of Scripture and of pre-Augustinian tradition (1) characterize the Logos and the Spirit directly only in their economic-soteriological function (respectively as truth, word, *etcetera*, and as love, gift, *etcetera*), and furthermore (2) do not show an unambiguously clear and steadily maintained attribution of these characterizations of the Father's economic self-communication to the Logos and the Spirit. For, in the light of our trinitarian basic axiom, the first consideration is in favor of such a "psychological" understanding of the two intra-divine processions. The second should not prevent us from accepting the conclusions from the first. This is so first of all because, from the very nature of the case, in both "economic" self-communications of God, he is given in his (essential) fullness. Hence both self-communications of God may be characterized by *all* (*at first* always) essential properties of God's spirituality.

Moreover, both of these intra-divine processions determine *each other*.[41] Hence it makes sense to affirm this mutual ordination of "generation" and knowledge on the one hand, of "spiration" of the Spirit and love on the other hand, even though we cannot further explain *why* and *how* these two basic actuations of God's essence, as present in the unoriginate Father and, on account of God's simplicity, essentially identical within him, constitute nonetheless the basis for two processions and thus for three distinct manners of subsisting.

2. PROBLEMS OF THEORY

That is where, in fact, the difficulties of the classic psychological speculations about the Trinity set in. They have no evident model *from* human psychology *for* the doctrine of the Trinity (a model known already before the doctrine of the Trinity), to explain why divine knowledge, as absolute primordial self-presence, necessarily means the distinct manner of subsisting of that which is "uttered." Or even why divine knowledge means an *utterance*, and not simply original self-presence in absolute identity.[42] Rather it postulates *from* the doctrine of the Trinity a model of human knowledge and love, which either remains questionable, or about which it is not clear that it can be more

---

41. This does not deny the τάξις of both processions, nor that the Spirit proceeds from the Father and (through) the Son, nor that we can*not* say that the Son proceeds from the Spirit. The statement simply emphasizes two points. First: there can exist in the absolutely simple and necessary God nothing which would be simply indifferent for some other "moment" in him. Every such moment exists *because* there is this God with all his other determinations. Next, for every metaphysics of the spirit even knowledge as such possesses already a moment of volition, hence of love. This too entails that the utterance of the Logos as such occurs in a movement of love, which reaches its completion in the "breathing" of the Spirit.

42. The same should be said about the Spirit as love.

than a *model* of human knowledge precisely as *finite*. And this model it applies again to God.[43] In other words, we are not told why in God knowledge and love demand a *processio ad modum operati* (as Word or as "the beloved in the lover"). The difficulty grows because we cannot say that the actual divine knowledge or love, insofar as either is the Father's as such (already given with his divine essence) are formally constituted by the Word. We cannot say, therefore, that the Father knows *through* the Word; rather he says the Word because he knows. If a human psychology can demand an *operatum* (an object of the act of knowing), it can do so only because and insofar as otherwise spiritual knowledge as such would not exist. Hence such a psychological theory of the Trinity will be meaningful only if it remains ever more clearly aware of the above mentioned circular reasoning, while building upon the positive insights which we have enumerated under (1). Then it becomes clear too that such a psychological theory of the Trinity has the character of what the other sciences call an "hypothesis."[44]

43. That was already basically the case with Augustine. Regarding the main basic concepts of the Augustinian doctrine of the Trinity, cp. the studies of U. Duchrow, *Sprachverständniss und biblisches Hören bei Augustin*, Tübingen, 1965, and A. Schindler, *Wort und Analogie in Augustins Trinitätslehre*, Tübingen, 1965. Both works offer plenty of materials and are based upon a solid knowledge of the literature. There remains now the task of drawing the practical consequences from these works.

44. Cp., for instance, the statements of Lonergan in volume I of *De Deo Trino*, pp. 276–298, and pp. 7–64 in volume II. They too ultimately amount only to a "hypothesis." A concrete evaluation of the different forms of the "psychological" doctrine of the Trinity would have to examine Lonergan's interpretation and further elaboration of St. Thomas (especially the concept of "verbum"). Concerning the problems cp. the following work which derives from the Lonergan school: R. L. Richard, *The Problem of an Apologetical Perspective in the Trinitarian Theology of St. Thomas Aquinas*, Rome, 1963, with literature.

3. METHODOLOGICAL DIFFICULTIES

The classical psychological doctrine of the Trinity suffers also from another methodological weakness. In its speculations it does not refer to what we know about the *origin* of the dogma of the "immanent" Trinity. When developing its ideas it has, as it were, forgotten about the "economic" Trinity.[45] If one does not do this, if one always remains within what faith tells about the "economic" Trinity, it is still possible to construct a "psychological" theology of the Trinity. We are not forced to stay only with abstract-formal statements about subsistence and so forth, as in the Eastern theology of the Trinity. We may build a psychological theology of the Trinity, even though such a theology is essentially more modest than the classic one in its design (not in its success), that is, even though it does not try to explain *why* divine knowledge and love imply two *processiones ad modum operati*. For in the "economic" doctrine of the Trinity we have understood God's self-communication as two-and-one in truth and love, as truth and love. If we experience that the divine self-communication is given in two distinct ways, then the two intradivine processions are already co-known as distinct in this experience of the faith, even though we cannot tell why they still remain such even when we abstract from the free "economic" aspect ("for us") of the "immanent" Trinity. We might even ask the further question (which we cannot go into here) whether it would not be possible to derive the "model" for a "psychological" doctrine of the Trinity not so much from an *abstract* consideration of the human spirit and its activities (in a strangely isolated individualism), but rather from those structures of human existence which first clearly appear in its experience of salvation

45. Precisely this impression is made, for example, by Lonergan's great two-volume work, *De Deo Trino*.

history: in its transcendence towards the future, as lovingly opening up and accepted; in its existence in history, in which the faithful truth is present as knowledge about itself.

G. On Features Peculiar to the Present Treatise

Let us emphasize once more that we could not help presenting in a very unsystematic way the "systematic" doctrine of the Trinity. We had to bypass some themes and underline others. We felt entitled to do so for two reasons. In the first place, there are a number of questions which, even though scholastic theology had displayed great conceptual subtleness regarding them, remain kerygmatically rather sterile. Secondly, as is evident from our basic axiom, Christology and the doctrine of grace *are*, strictly speaking, doctrine of the Trinity. They are its two chapters about either divine procession or mission ("immanent" and "economic"). Hence what we have already presented here is and intends to be nothing more than a certain formal anticipation of Christology and pneumatology (doctrine of grace) which are to follow. In order to understand them, we must emphasize in Christology the dogma that "only" the Logos became man and that this manifests him *as* such. We must emphasize the insight that this was obviously not due to a random "decree" of God, who might also have decided the incarnation of another divine person. Further, in pneumatology, we must construct a doctrine of grace which possesses a trinitarian structure. When all this happens, then the real doctrine of the Trinity is presented in Christology and in pneumatology.

Even so, not a few questions and answers had unfortunately to be bypassed. On the other hand, nothing that the Bible or revelation or kerygmatic necessity invited us to say about the Trinity was overlooked in the "systematic" discussion of the present dogmatic essay.

INDEX OF TOPICS

OTHER WRITINGS BY KARL RAHNER
ON THE TRINITY

"The Concept of Mystery in Catholic Theology," *Theological Investigations*, vol. 4, trans. K. Smyth (New York: Crossroad, 1982), 36-73.

"God," "God, Attributes of," "Trinity, Divine," in *Sacramentum Mundi: An Encyclopedia of Theology* (New York: Herder & Herder, 1968-70), vol. 2, 381-99; vol. 2, 399-401; vol. 6, 295-303.

"An Investigation of the Incomprehensibility of God in St. Thomas Aquinas," *Theological Investigations*, vol. 16, trans. D. Morland (New York: Crossroad, 1976), 244-54.

"The Mystery of the Trinity," *Theological Investigations*, vol. 16, trans. D. Morland (New York: Crossroad, 1976), 255-59.

"Remarks on the Dogmatic Treatise 'De Trinitate,'" *Theological Investigations*, vol. 4, trans. K. Smyth (New York: Crossroad, 1982), 77-102.

"Theos in the New Testament," *Theological Investigations*, vol. 1, trans. C. Ernst (New York: Crossroad, 1982), 79-148.